BIBLE

TIC TAC TOE

BIBLE

TIC TAC TOE

DONNA K. MALTESE

BARBOUR
PUBLISHING

© 2011 by Barbour Publishing, Inc.

ISBN 978-1-60260-896-2

All rights reserved. No part of this publication may be reproduced or transmitted for commercial purposes, except for brief quotations in printed reviews, without written permission of the publisher.

Churches and other noncommercial interests may reproduce portions of this book without the express written permission of Barbour Publishing, provided that the text does not exceed 500 words and that the text is not material quoted from another publisher. When reproducing text from this book, include the following credit line: "From *Bible Tic-Tac-Toe*, published by Barbour Publishing, Inc. Used by permission."

Scripture quotations marked NIV are taken from the HOLY BIBLE, NEW INTERNATIONAL VERSION®. NIV®. Copyright © 1973, 1978, 1984, 2011 by Biblica, Inc.™. Used by permission. All rights reserved worldwide.

Scripture quotations marked CEV are from the Contemporary English Version, Copyright © 1991, 1992, 1995 by American Bible Society. Used by permission.

Scripture quotations marked KJV are taken from the King James Version of the Bible.

Scripture quotations marked NKJV are taken from the New King James Version®. Copyright © 1982 by Thomas Nelson, Inc. Used by permission. All rights reserved.

Scripture quotations marked NASB are taken from the New American Standard Bible, © 1960, 1962, 1963, 1968, 1971, 1972, 1973, 1975, 1977, 1995 by The Lockman Foundation. Used by permission.

Scripture quotations marked NCV are taken from the New Century Version, copyright © 2005 by Thomas Nelson, Inc. Used by permission.

Scripture quotations marked AMP are taken from the Amplified® Bible, © 1954, 1958, 1962, 1964, 1965, 1987 by The Lockman Foundation. Used by permission.

Scripture quotations marked NLT are taken from the *Holy Bible*, New Living Translation copyright © 1996, 2004, 2007 by Tyndale House Foundation. Used by permission of Tyndale House Publishers, Inc. Carol Stream, Illinois 60188. All rights reserved.

Scripture quotations marked MSG are from THE MESSAGE. Copyright © by Eugene H. Peterson 1993, 1994, 1995, 1996, 2000, 2001, 2002. Used by permission of NavPress Publishing Group.

Published by Barbour Publishing, Inc., P.O. Box 719, Uhrichsville, Ohio 44683, www.barbourbooks.com

Our mission is to publish and distribute inspirational products offering exceptional value and biblical encouragement to the masses.

 Member of the
Evangelical Christian
Publishers Association

Printed in the United States of America.

Welcome to
BIBLE Tic-Tac-Toe...

. . .a game that will provide you with many hours of challenge and fun! Each of these fifty interactive quizzes will test your knowledge of scripture with trivia questions that, when answered correctly, will entitle you to put an *X* or an *O* in a spot within the three-by-three square grid. The book is set up so that you can play the games by yourself or against an opponent. Or, better yet, use it in your Sunday school classes, allowing children and adults alike to have fun competing as they test each other on Bible knowledge!

Each quiz features nine questions of average difficulty in a multiple-choice format, though occasionally you'll come across a question that is easier or harder than average. When you think you know the answer, check to make sure you're right! You can find the correct answer to each question in the back of this book, in the answer key. The answers are arranged by the question number in each quiz. So, for instance, to find the answer to question 3 in quiz 23, turn to the section titled "Question 3" and scroll down to quiz 23 for the correct answer. Each answer also includes the scripture reference the answer comes from.

When you succeed in answering a question correctly, you can place either an *X* or an *O* in any box on the grid. When you have three of the respective marks in a row—either horizontally, vertically, or diagonally—you win the game, whether or not you've answered all the questions in the quiz! If, after going through the entire quiz, you (or you and your opponent) have not gotten three of the same marks in a row, count up how many *X*s and *O*s are on the entire grid. Whoever has the most marks wins!

If you are playing against an opponent, remember your tic-tac-toe strategies. When possible, you can try to block your opponent from making a complete row. You can also try to threaten your opponent by placing your marks so that you can win with a possible completion in two different directions. Remember to take turns. For example, if you, designated as *X*, take question 1 and answer correctly, place an *X* in any square on the grid. Then allow *O* to take his or her turn with question 2. If you answer question 1 incorrectly, you do not make a mark in the grid, and *O* goes on to question number 2, and so on.

So, are you up for the challenge? Are you ready to tackle *Bible Tic-Tac-Toe*? If so, put on your thinking cap, grab a sharp pencil, and begin with any quiz in the book. And remember. . . if you get stumped on a question, you can always try doing what Saul did. He "prayed to God, 'O God of Israel. . . Show me the truth.' " (1 Samuel 14:41 MSG).

Quiz 1

Greetings! Since we're starting at the beginning, I thought it only fitting that I—Adam, the first man ever created—guide you through quiz number 1. But be careful where you step. We're not in the garden anymore, so there are snares galore. Are you ready to raise Cain? If so, let's go!

1. God made the sun on which day of creation?
    a. second
    b. third
    c. fourth
    d. Sunday

2. What tree did God tell Adam he was not to eat from?
    a. the tree in the middle of the garden
    b. the tree of life
    c. the tree of knowledge of good and evil
    d. the tree of diamonds

3. After Cain killed his brother Abel, Eve gave birth to Seth. What was the name of Seth's son?
    a. Enosh
    b. Kenan
    c. Enoch
    d. Rogen

4. In Romans 5:14, Paul wrote that "death reigned from the time of Adam to the time of" *whom*?
    a. Methuselah
    b. Moses
    c. Elisha
    d. Christ

5. When the sons of God went to the daughters of men, they had children known as *what*?
    a. Cherubim
    b. Seraphim
    c. Halflings
    d. Nephilim

6. Noah was known as what kind of man?
   a. incorruptible
   b. a sailor
   c. righteous
   d. an arkonaut

7. Nimrod was a mighty warrior. What was his father's name?
   a. Cush
   b. Canaan
   c. Nabal the fool
   d. Lightning Rod

8. Noah had three sons. Two of them were named Shem and Japheth. What was the third one's name?

   a. Canaan
   b. Lamech
   c. Ham
   d. Bologna

9. The tower of Babel was located in the plain in *where*?
   a. Spain
   b. Mesha
   c. Sephar
   d. Shinar

Quiz 1—Wrap-up

Congratulations on completing the first quiz. And kudos to you if you answered all your questions correctly. Right now, I've got to run. Eve's calling me in to dinner. Hope it's not forbidden fruit again! Those seeds always seem to get caught in my teeth. May God be with you as you continue your journey through this book—and beyond.

"As long as the earth endures, seedtime and harvest,
cold and heat, summer and winter,
day and night will never cease."
GENESIS 8:22 NIV

Quiz 2

Hello there, stranger. My name is Abraham, and I'll be your guide through quiz 2. Great things will be coming our way as we travel through the next nine questions. But be cautious with your answers. We're not in Ur anymore.

1. Abraham's wife Sarai (aka Sarah) was also *what*?
    a. Pharocious
    b. Lot's niece
    c. a princess
    d. Abraham's sister

2. During a famine, Abraham went *where*?
    a. Greece
    b. Egypt
    c. Acme
    d. Rome

3. When Lot and Abraham parted, Lot pitched his tents near *where*?

    a. right
    b. wrong
    c. Gomorrah
    d. Sodom

4. After rescuing Lot from villainous kings, Abraham met a priest named Melchizedek, who was the king of *what*?
    a. Sodom
    b. Canaan
    c. Salem
    d. the road

5. In the New Testament, James wrote that "Abraham believed God, and it was credited to him as" *what*?
    a. righteousness
    b. a bankable asset
    c. a man of good standing
    d. great faith

6. Peter said that "Sarah obeyed Abraham and called him her" *what*?
   a. husband
   b. master
   c. helpmate
   d. patriarchic duty

7. In Luke 16, Jesus tells a story about a rich man who goes to hell and, looking across a chasm, sees by Abraham's side *whom*?
   a. Mary Todd
   b. the leper Simon
   c. the beggar Lazarus
   d. the tax collector Matthew

8. Near the great trees of Mamre, Abraham was sitting at the door when he saw how many men approaching?
   a. one
   b. three
   c. seven
   d. ten

9. Abraham was *what* when he died?
   a. single
   b. assassinated
   c. 175 years old
   d. the father of many sons

Quiz 2—Wrap-up

I hope you had as much fun on this journey as I've had on all of mine. No matter where you are in life, never forget that God is just waiting to bless you. All you need to do is obey—like I did (well, most of the time anyway). May His heavenly host watch over you!

> *"The Lord, before whom I have walked faithfully,*
> *will send his angel with you and*
> *make your journey a success."*
> GENESIS 24:40 NIV

Quiz 3

Welcome to quiz 3. I'm Sarah, Abraham's wife. My plans have been known to backfire, but I think we'll get through the next nine questions with flying colors—just make sure you follow the leading of the Holy Spirit instead of walking in *my* sandals. For with the Spirit as your guide, you're certain to come out victorious! Ready? Set? Let's go!

1. After God told Abraham he'd have many sons, Sarah still remained barren. So, taking things into her own hands, she had Abraham marry her maid named *what*?

   a. Hazel
   b. Keturah
   c. Hagar
   d. Concepción

2. After Sarah's pregnant maid fled from her mistress's presence, she sat down at a well and cried. Following God's appearance to her there, the well was named *Beer Lahai Roi*, which means *what*?

   a. You Are the God Who Sees
   b. Well of Fortune
   c. Place of Weeping
   d. Spring of God's Presence

3. When Sarah overheard the Lord telling her husband that she and Abraham, both well past child-bearing age, would have their own son, she did *what*?

   a. jumped for joy
   b. laughed
   c. cried
   d. had a mental pause

4. How old were Abraham, Ishmael, and Isaac when they were circumcised?

   a. old enough to have a camel-driver's license
   b. 101 years, 15 years, and 8 weeks, respectively
   c. 100 years, 14 years, and 10 days, respectively
   d. 99 years, 13 years, and 8 days, respectively

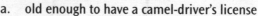

5. The Lord told Abraham to sacrifice Isaac *where*?

    a. Hill of Golgotha
    b. Sheephead Mountain
    c. Region of Moriah
    d. Mount Horeb

6. When the Lord enabled Abraham to sacrifice a ram instead of his son Isaac, he called the name of that place *what*?

    a. The Lord Will Save Us
    b. God Has Heard My Cry
    c. The Lord Will Provide
    d. Mount of Wool Gatherers

7. In Romans 4:19, Paul writes, "Without weakening in his faith, [Abraham] faced the fact that his body was as good as dead—since he was" about how many years old?

    a. 95   c. 105
    b. 100   d. 110

8. In Galatians 4:22, Paul writes, "Abraham had two sons, one by the slave woman and the other by" *whom*?

    a. "the free woman"
    b. "Sarah, a woman of faith"
    c. "the woman who released laughter"
    d. "a woman loosed"

9. After Sarah died, at the age of 127, Abraham buried her in the cave of the field of *what*?

    a. Heth   c. Hebron
    b. Sorrow   d. Machpelah

Quiz 3—Wrap-up

Whew! Was that easy or tough? If the former, you're an excellent Bible student. If the latter, you may need to brush up from Genesis to Revelation. Meanwhile, remember that no matter how complicated our situations may be, we would be wise not to run ahead of God's plan. Because He always knows what's best for us! That's a lesson I had to learn the hard way.

"I am the LORD!
There is nothing too difficult for me."
GENESIS 18:14 CEV

Quiz 4

Hi! Lot here. Ready to handle the next batch of questions? You may need a "lot" of help. But then again, maybe you'll do fine on your own. That's what I tried to do. Away from Uncle Abraham, I attempted to hoe my own row. That's when I got into a lot of trouble. I hope you make better choices in this quiz—either by yourself or against an opponent—than I did in life. Either way, may God go with you—and you with God—as you tackle these questions.

1. Lot's dad was named *what*?
   - a. Acre
   - b. Eber
   - c. Haran
   - d. Reu

2. In Genesis 14:1, the king of Elam, along with a few other kings, took Lot captive. What was this king's name?
   - a. Amraphel
   - b. Kedorlaomer
   - c. Tidal
   - d. Realtor

3. When two angels came to rescue Lot before Sodom was destroyed, what was Abraham's nephew doing?
   - a. playing Monopoly
   - b. selling his wares
   - c. sitting at the gate
   - d. preparing a fatted calf for dinner

4. When villainous men began attacking Lot's house, the angels did *what*?
   - a. kept really quiet until the men went away
   - b. drew "lots" to see who would go outside and fight the villains
   - c. smote the men to smithereens
   - d. struck the men with blindness so they couldn't find the front door

5. What happened to Lot's wife when she disobeyed the angels and looked back at Sodom?
   - a. She was hit with pepper spray
   - b. She became a pillar of salt
   - c. She was blinded
   - d. She was buried under ash

6. Right after Sodom was destroyed, Lot ran to what city?
   - a. Shur
   - b. Gerar
   - c. Zoar
   - d. Siddimdown

7. When describing the Second Coming, as recorded in Luke 17:32, Jesus said, "No one in the field should go back for anything. Remember" *what*?
   - a. "the Alamo!"
   - b. "the pillar of salt!"
   - c. "Lot's race to the caves of Gerar!"
   - d. "Lot's wife!"

8. In 2 Peter 2:7–8 (NIV), Peter writes that Lot, while living among the lawless people of Sodom, was *what*?

   - a. "morally upright"
   - b. "entertaining angels"
   - c. "tormented in his righteous soul"
   - d. "backsliding"

9. While hiding in a cave, Lot's daughters procured sons by their father. These two sons and/or grandsons by Lot became the progenitors of what peoples?
   - a. Moabites and Ammonites
   - b. Hittites and Amorites
   - c. Canaanites and Perizzites
   - d. Stalagmites and Stalactites

Quiz 4—Wrap-up

Well, I hope you've had lots of fun with this quiz. And
always remember to follow God's leading, not your own.
For the grass is *not* always greener on the other side of the
fence—or on the plain of the Jordan, for that matter. *Ciao*
for now!

> *Trust in the LORD with all your heart,*
> *and lean not on your own understanding;*
> *in all your ways acknowledge Him,*
> *and He shall direct your paths.*
> PROVERBS 3:5–6 NKJV

Quiz 5

Greetings! My name is Isaac. You may already have met my parents, Abraham and Sarah. They were pretty old by the time they had me. Talk about a generation gap! Although many years spanned between us, my folks taught me a lot about God and faith. I hope you learn something, too, as you attempt to master this quiz!

1. God fulfilled His promise made to Abraham and Sarah with the birth of their son Isaac, whose name means *what*?
    - a. promise
    - b. blessing
    - c. It's about time!
    - d. laughter

2. Before sending his servant off to find a wife for his son, Abraham made the man swear not to choose a wife for Isaac from among the daughters of the Canaanites. As confirmation of his pledge, the servant did *what*?
    - a. He placed a kiss on both of Abraham's cheeks.
    - b. He shook hands with Abraham.
    - c. He placed his hand beneath Abraham's thigh.
    - d. He spit on ten camels.

3. What was the name of Rebekah's brother?
    - a. Laban
    - b. Nahor
    - c. Bethuel
    - d. Hermano

4. How old was Isaac when he married Rebekah?
    - a. thirty
    - b. thirty-five
    - c. forty
    - d. fifty

5. When the once-barren Rebekah was pregnant, the children inside her tussled with each other. So she asked the Lord why this was so. What was God's response?
    - a. "There's not enough womb."
    - b. "Your sons will struggle."
    - c. "You will give birth to twins."
    - d. "Two nations are in your womb."

6. Esau, Isaac's son, bore a grudge against his twin brother, Jacob, because from Esau Jacob stole *what*?
   a. his wife
   b. his sheep
   c. his dune buggy
   d. his father's blessing

7. Quoting from Genesis 21:12, in Romans 9:7 (NIV) Paul wrote that God told Abraham, "It is through Isaac that your offspring will" *what*?

   a. "be reckoned"
   b. "be related"
   c. "jump forth"
   d. "rule"

8. In Galatians 4:28 (NIV), Paul wrote, "Now you, brothers and sisters, like Isaac, are children of" *what*?
   a. "Father Abraham"
   b. "the Lord God"
   c. "promise"
   d. "Mayan"

9. Esau had three wives. Two were named Judith and Basemath, and the third was named *what*?
   a. Highermath
   b. Mahalath
   c. Nebaioth
   d. Dinah

Quiz 5—Wrap-up

I hope you enjoyed playing this game! Speaking of "game," I love eating it when it's savory. Unfortunately, one of my sons used that knowledge for his own benefit, which created a very hairy situation for my entire family. I must've been blind not to see what was happening. But that's a whole 'nother story, and I've got to run. So, see you later! And God bless!

> *"I am the God of your father Abraham;*
> *do not fear, for I am with you.*
> *I will bless you."*
> GENESIS 26:24 NKJV

Quiz 6

How do you do? They call me Jacob. And, boy, do I have some stories for you! But I'm not sure I have enough time to tell you every one. So I'll be quizzing you on how well you know me and my *huge* family. But watch out! Some things are not quite the way they seem.

1. The name Jacob means *what*?
   a. pretender
   b. planter
   c. corn
   d. heel-catcher

2. After deceiving his father, Isaac, Jacob ran off to *where*?
   a. Paddan Aram
   b. Holy Wood
   c. Gerar
   d. Canaan

3. After dreaming of a stairway to heaven, Jacob renamed the place where he'd slept Bethel, which had previously been called *what*?

   a. Haran
   b. Serta
   c. Luz
   d. Penuel

4. Jacob fell in love with Rachel and was tricked into marrying Leah. Later he also married Rachel's maid and Leah's maid, the latter of whom was named *what*?
   a. Hagar
   b. Bilhah
   c. Marian
   d. Zilpah

5. Which of the following were two of the eleven children borne to Jacob by Leah?
   a. Gad and Asher
   b. Dan and Naphtali
   c. Issachar and Zebulun
   d. Levi and Strauss

6. In Genesis 30:37 (NIV), what kind of fresh-cut tree branches did Jacob put before the sheep in an attempt to make them speckled, spotted, or brown?
   a. poplar, almond, and plane
   b. olive, oak, and elm
   c. fig, pomegranate, and mulberry
   d. birch, juniper, and chestnut

7. Jacob struggled with God in Mahanaim, and because the now-limping Jacob prevailed, the battle site was renamed Peniel, which means *what*?

   a. Place of Victory
   b. Double Camp
   c. Pork Chop Hill
   d. Face of God

8. Psalm 105:23 states, "Jacob resided as a foreigner in the land of" *what*?
   a. Ham
   b. Egypt
   c. Canaan
   d. Oz

9. In Isaiah 41:14, what descriptive insect-like term is used before the name *Jacob* to denote Israel's feeble and hated condition in exile?
   a. maggot
   b. worm
   c. fly
   d. gnat

Quiz 6—Wrap-up

Gee, we've covered topics from corn to maggots. I hope you had a good time. I'll sign off now as another patriarch, who's also a favorite relative of mine, is ready to take over. So, keep smiling because the fun continues!

Happy is he who has the God of Jacob for his help,
Whose hope is in the LORD his God.
PSALM 146:5 NKJV

Quiz 7

Shalom! I'm Joseph, the eldest son of Rachel and Jacob, and I'm here to introduce quiz 7, where you'll encounter everything from Asher to Zebulun (those are the names of two of my brothers—well, half brothers, anyway). So get your pencil sharpened, ready to mark some Xs and Os. Here we go!

1. Which of Joseph's half brothers killed Shechem, the man who raped their sister Dinah, and his father, Hamor?

    a. Reuben and Issachar
    b. Asher and Zebulun
    c. Levi and Simeon
    d. Abraham and Strauss

2. Which of Judah's sons was the last one married to the soon-to-be-twice-widowed Tamar?

    a. Onan
    b. Er
    c. Shelah
    d. Earl E. Demise

3. Which of Joseph's ten brothers talked the others out of killing him?
    a. Levi   c. Reuben
    b. Judah   d. Pax

4. While in prison, Joseph interpreted the dreams of two of Pharaoh's servants. Which one lived to serve again?
    a. cupbearer
    b. butcher
    c. baker
    d. candlestick maker

5. Joseph was imprisoned in Egypt. Three other biblical characters were imprisoned in Jerusalem, one of whom was named *what*?
    a. Dr. Richard Kimble
    b. Jeremiah
    c. Silas
    d. Zedekiah

6. Pharaoh dreamed of cows and heads of grain. What number of each did he dream?
   - a. three
   - b. four
   - c. seven
   - d. in-cow-culable

7. Which one of Joseph's sons received a blessing from Jacob's right hand, thus foretelling the dominance of one son's tribe over the other?
   - a. Zaphnath
   - b. Ephraim
   - c. Manasseh
   - d. Usurper

8. As he lay dying, Joseph gave directions about *what*?
   - a. his burial site
   - b. his sons
   - c. his bones
   - d. his GPS (Guidance per the Spirit)

9. In Revelation 7:8, how many of the tribe of Joseph were sealed?
   - a. 12,000
   - b. 24,000
   - c. 144,000
   - d. undisclosed

Quiz 7—Wrap-up

So, did that quiz tickle your Tic-Tac-*Toes*? If not, I hope you don't feel de-*feet*-ed. Because no matter what, we have victory in God! You can be assured of that!

> *But thanks be to God! He gives us the victory through our Lord Jesus Christ.*
> 1 CORINTHIANS 15:57 NIV

Quiz 8

Hey there, gamer. Moses here, and I've got nine good questions for you. Originally, I wrote them all down on a tablet—that's a habit of mine—and I've rewritten them here, just for you. We'll start out in Exodus, a wild journey into the wilderness, and eventually settle into the Promised Land—some of us, anyway. So if you're ready to begin, let's wander on down the page, starting with question 1.

1. After murdering an Egyptian, Moses fled to where?

   a. Sinai
   b. Midian
   c. Kadesh Barnea
   d. OshKosh b'Goshen

2. Gershom's grandmother (aka Moses' mom) was named *what*?
   a. Shiphrah   c. Jochebed
   b. Zipporah   d. Grandma Moses

3. Moses's father-in-law, Jethro, was known by what other name?
   a. Reuel   c. Ithamar
   b. Amram   d. Bodine

4. By the burning bush in Exodus 4, God gave Moses miraculous signs to convince the Israelites he was God's chosen leader. Which one is *not* one of those three initial powers?
   a. staff turning into a snake and back again
   b. bringing forth gnats to cover men and beasts
   c. hand turning leprous and then healing
   d. pouring water from the Nile onto the dry ground, where it changed into blood

5. In 2 Timothy 3:8 (NASB), Paul mentions two magicians who opposed Moses by using their sacred arts to imitate the prophets' miracles. What were their names?
   a. Siegfried and Roy
   b. Putiel and Phineas
   c. Korah and Kohath
   d. Jannes and Jambres

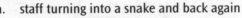

6. Which of Moses' miracles were Pharaoh's magicians *not* able to imitate?
    a. bringing forth gnats to cover men and beasts
    b. changing their staffs into snakes
    c. turning water into blood
    d. making frogs come up over the land

7. In what bitter waters did Moses throw a stick to make the water drinkable?
    a. Brita
    b. Elim
    c. Rephidim
    d. Marah

8. In 2 Corinthians 3:15 (NIV), Paul wrote that "when Moses is read," something covers the Israelites' hearts. What is that something?
    a. "the people's sins"
    b. "a veil"
    c. "waters of de Nile"
    d. "Christ's blood"

9. Disputing with the devil about the body of Moses was *who*?
    a. Aaron
    b. Joshua
    c. Michael the archangel
    d. Daniel Webster

Quiz 8—Wrap-up

Still having fun? Some of those questions were doozies! I hope you enjoyed answering them as much as I enjoyed writing them. Oh, wait a minute. My brother Aaron is waiting to test you. So I guess I'd better go. You know, Aaron may be a good speaker, but I think I write better than he does. We all have our talents, don't we? The trick is not to waste the gifts God gives us but use them in service to Him. That bit of wisdom is a little present from me to you! May the Lord bless you and keep you!

Moses summoned Bezalel and Oholiab along with all whom God had gifted with the ability to work skillfully with their hands. The men were eager to get started and engage in the work.
EXODUS 36:2 MSG

Quiz 9

Aaron here. I'm known as the "other brother." But I had a big role in helping our people get to the Promised Land, although Moses and I both died before we stepped foot in it. Anyway, I've been called to take you through quiz 9. So hold on to your camels. It's going to be a bumpy ride!

1. What was the name of Aaron's wife?
   a. Huldah
   b. Elisheba
   c. Rizpah
   d. Mrs. Burr

2. According to God's instructions, which one of the following colors of yarn was to be included in the ephod for Aaron?
   a. green
   b. yellow
   c. blue
   d. calfskin brown

3. Which of the following were the sons of Aaron who were killed because they offered unauthorized fire before the Lord?
   a. Nadab and Abihu
   b. Eleazar and Phinehas
   c. Ithamar and Eleazar
   d. Pyro and Maniac

4. How many hammered-silver trumpets did the Lord command Moses to make to call the community together and for having the camps set out?
   a. two
   b. seven
   c. twelve
   d. twenty-toot

5. For forty years, the Israelites ate manna, a word that means *what*?
   a. bread from heaven
   b. Is this wonder bread?
   c. the Lord provides
   d. What is it?

6. The Israelites grew sick of manna, craved and begged
    for meat, and got and ate quail. Afterward, some were
    struck with a plague and died. They named that site
    what?
    a. Hazeroth
    b. Kibroth Hattaavah
    c. Taberah
    d. Mannayuck

7. After Miriam and Aaron opposed Moses because of his
    Cushite wife, Miriam *what*?
    a. became covered with boils
    b. was struck by fire from the Lord
    c. became leprous
    d. was confined to her tent for the remainder of
        the trip

8. Korah, Dathan, and Abiram, the three men who "rose"
    up against Moses, ended up being *what*?
    a. beaten with thorns
    b. killed, along with their families, by the
        Levites
    c. stoned to death
    d. swallowed up by the earth

9. Among the items Hebrews 9:4 lists as things contained
    in the ark, which of the following was *not* included?
    a. gold jar of manna
    b. bread of the Presence
    c. stone tablets of the covenant
    d. Aaron's staff

Quiz 9—Wrap-up

Well, as you can see, we had lots of adventures when we were in the desert. But we finally got to the land of milk and honey. More on that in another quiz. For now, remember that the Lord wants us to fellowship with Him no matter where we journey. For He truly cares for us. So, drop whatever you're doing, and spend a few minutes with Him right now.

> *"I carried you on eagles' wings*
> *and brought you to myself."*
> EXODUS 19:4 NIV

Quiz 10

Eleazar, Aaron's son, here! I took over the tabernacle duties when my brothers were "fired" for dereliction of duty. Anyway, Uncle Moses thought I might have some good questions for you. So, let's pull the curtain back and begin!

1. After sprouting, budding, and blooming, what type of fruit did Aaron's staff produce?
    a. figs
    b. almonds
    c. pomegranates
    d. Aaronuts

2. Eleazar's aunt Miriam died *where*?
    a. Rephidim
    b. Marah
    c. Kadesh
    d. Auntapolis

3. Who denied the wandering Israelites passage through their land?
    a. Edomites
    b. Moabites
    c. Ammonites
    d. Detourites

4. Eleazar's dad, Aaron, died *where*?
    a. Mount Toomuch
    b. Mount Sinai
    c. Mount Horeb
    d. Mount Hor

5. Moses and Aaron were refused entry into the Promised Land because they *what*?
    a. burned up a sin offering instead of eating it as the Lord commanded
    b. rebelled against the Lord's command at the waters of Meribah
    c. offered profane fire before the Lord
    d. didn't have passports

6. The name of the father of Balak, king of Moab, was *what*?
   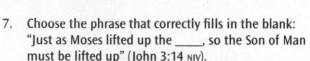
   a. Zippor
   b. Button
   c. Beor
   d. Zophim

7. Choose the phrase that correctly fills in the blank: "Just as Moses lifted up the _____, so the Son of Man must be lifted up" (John 3:14 NIV).
   a. ark of the covenant
   b. waters of the Red Sea
   c. manna from heaven
   d. snake in the wilderness

8. The son of Eleazar who continued the priestly line was named *what*?
   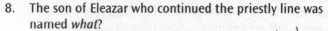
   a. Izhar
   b. Gershon
   c. Phinehas
   d. Pope

9. Taking over the leadership of the Israelites after Moses died was *who*?
   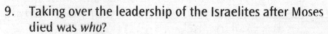
   a. Eleazar
   b. Joshua
   c. Golda Meir
   d. David

Quiz 10—Wrap-up

Well, speaking as a priest, I hope this quiz ministered to you. And remember, no matter how great the opposition, God is here to give us strength and courage as we leave the desert of sin behind and head into the Promised Land. I know. I've seen Him in action! Haven't you?

"Don't worry! The Lord our God will lead the way.
He will fight on our side, just as he did when we saw him
do all those things to the Egyptians. And you know that
the Lord has taken care of us the whole time we've been
in the desert, just as you might carry one of your children."
DEUTERONOMY 1:29–31 CEV

Quiz 11

Greetings! My name is Caleb. I was one of the spies Moses sent out to survey the Promised Land. When we returned, Josh and I gave a good report—unlike the others who went with us. So, as you work your way through this quiz, be like me: check out the lay of the land, and then take courage as you choose your answers. And perhaps at the end of it all, you'll give me a good report!

1. The tribe given the six cities of refuge to which a person who had killed someone could flee until trial was named *what*?

   a. Lawyerites
   b. Benjamites
   c. Levites
   d. Jebusites

2. Which was the last of the Ten Commandments?
   a. Honor your mom and dad.
   b. Do not covet.
   c. Do not bear false witness.
   d. Wash behind your ears.

3. Which one of the "foods" listed below did the Lord tell the Israelites they *could* eat?

   a. crickets
   b. geckoes
   c. eagles
   d. goobers

4. How many witnesses are needed to convict a man of a crime or offense?
   a. one or two
   b. two or three
   c. three or four
   d. twelve angry men

5. Joshua was the son of Nun. Caleb was the son of *whom*?
   a. Rambow
   b. Dathan
   c. Eliab
   d. Jephunneh

6. Before he died, Moses viewed the Promised Land from Mount *what*?
   a. Sinai
   b. Horeb
   c. Nebo
   d. Renege

7. The land Joshua gave Caleb as his inheritance, because the latter had followed the Lord wholeheartedly, was called *what*?
   a. Old Faithful
   b. Hebron
   c. Debir
   d. Heshbon

8. The name of Caleb's daughter who was offered in marriage to the man who attacked and captured Kiriath Sepher was *what*?
   a. Trophiwifeh
   b. Ephrath
   c. Maacah
   d. Acsah

9. The name of the man who won Caleb's daughter's hand was *what*?
   a. Othniel
   b. Kenaz
   c. Jesher
   d. Groomer

Quiz 11—Wrap-up

Hope you didn't have to battle too hard through that quiz.
Take it from a man who was, at times, battle weary.
But I never gave up, never stopped following the Lord,
because I always knew where to find Him. Do you?

> "If. . .you seek the LORD your God, you will find him
> if you seek him with all your heart
> and with all your soul."
> DEUTERONOMY 4:29 NIV

Quiz 12

A hallowed hello to you from me, Joshua the son of Nun. Welcome to the Promised Land! Whew! We finally made it. But it took some doing. Especially after our arrival, when we had lots of battles to fight. But I don't want to give away the whole story. So grab a sharp pencil and get the lead out. There's no time to lose!

1. Numbers 13:16 says that Moses gave the son of Nun the name *Joshua*. Joshua's original name was *what*?
    a. Nil
    b. Shaphat
    c. Hori
    d. Hoshea

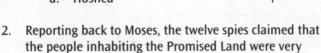

2. Reporting back to Moses, the twelve spies claimed that the people inhabiting the Promised Land were very strong and tall. These giant people were called *what*?
    a. Bunyanites
    b. Anakites
    c. Ammonites
    d. Rephidites

3. The phrase found four times in Joshua 1 is *what*?

    a. "No swimming in the Jordan."
    b. "Do not be discouraged."
    c. "Be strong."
    d. "Do not be afraid."

4. The prostitute Rahab of Jericho hid Joshua's spies *where*?
    a. in the well
    b. under stalks of flax
    c. in a cave
    d. at a "rahab" center

5. In what town did the waters of Jordan pile up in a heap, allowing the Israelites to cross on dry land?
    a. Zarethan
    b. Jericho
    c. Waverly
    d. Adam

6. What man's taking of booty from Jericho caused the Israelites to be defeated when they first attempted to take the city of Ai?
   a. Blackbeard
   b. Zimri
   c. Zerah
   d. Achan

7. The supernatural miracle God performed to help Joshua and his men successfully defend the Gibeonites was *what*?

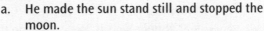

   a. He made the sun stand still and stopped the moon.
   b. He struck the enemy soldiers with a plague.
   c. He divided the waters of the Jordan.
   d. He infested the land with gibbons.

8. The town Joshua received as his inheritance was *what*?
   a. Beth Anath
   b. Ekron
   c. Timnath Serah
   d. Joshtown

9. Joshua's most famous quote was "Choose for yourselves this day whom you will serve. . . . As for me and my" *what* "we will serve the Lord"?
   a. family
   b. household
   c. people
   d. shadow

Quiz 12—Wrap-up

Well, I guess that about covers it. Hope you won this game! I promise the next one will be even better. And I, like God, keep my promises. But you be the judge. Come to think of it, that's who's hosting the next game! An Israelite judge! So, get ready. 'Cause here comes the judge!

> *Not a single one of all the good promises the Lord had given to the family of Israel was left unfulfilled; everything he had spoken came true.*
> Joshua 21:45 NLT

Quiz 13

Please rise—court is in session! My name is Deborah, and I was not only the fourth judge of Israel and wife of Lappidoth but a prophetess as well. Pretty cool, huh? I'm here to introduce quiz 13. These questions will test your knowledge of the book of Judges. So let's get started.

1. The first three judges of Israel were *who*?
    a. Judith, Mathis, and Ito
    b. Gideon, Tola, and Jair
    c. Othniel, Ehud, and Shamgar
    d. Ibzan, Elon, and Abdon

2. During Deborah's judgeship, who was the commander of the Israelites' army?
    a. Rakkath
    b. Barak
    c. Makir
    d. Shaq

3. The woman named Jael killed Sisera, the Canaanite army commander, *how*?
    a. She hung him after a lengthy "Jael" term.
    b. She drove a sword through his abdomen.
    c. She had him trampled by a herd of camels.
    d. She drove a tent peg through his temple.

4. Seeking a sign from God, Gideon, the fifth judge of Israel, set out on the threshing floor *what*?
    a. a trumpet
    b. "chaff" stick
    c. a fleece
    d. an altar

5. In paring down Gideon's army, God ordered Gideon to take into battle the three hundred men who *what*?
    a. lapped like dogs
    b. drank like camels
    c. ate like birds
    d. swam like fish

6. Gideon's son, who became Israel's first self-declared king, was named *what*?
   a. Jerub-Baal
   b. Jotham
   c. Abimelech
   d. Elvis

7. Jephthah was a mighty warrior who made a "rash" vow to the Lord, which resulted in *what*?
   a. a chronic itch
   b. the loss of his wife
   c. leprosy for life
   d. the sacrifice of his daughter

8. The strongman Samson had a relative named *what*?

   a. Zorah
   b. Manoah
   c. Hillel
   d. Samsonite

9. When Delilah first asked Samson the secret of his strength, he told her he'd become weak if *what*?
   a. he didn't have his Wheaties
   b. he was tied with new ropes
   c. his hair was shorn
   d. he was tied with seven fresh bowstrings

Quiz 13—Wrap-up

Wow! Talk about a strong finish! I hope you had a good time with this quiz. If you found it difficult, don't judge yourself too harshly. There's always the next quiz—and that one won't be *ruth*less. Meanwhile, have a safe trip as you make your way through these puzzles. And God bless.

> *"Go in peace. . . . For the LORD is watching over your journey."*
> JUDGES 18:6 NLT

Quiz 14

The Lord bless you! Ruth here. And, boy, do I have a great quiz for you! Have you heard the story about me and my mother-in-law, Naomi? It's a good one. And I hope you know it well. For that knowledge will help you answer the next nine questions. So, don't turn back now. Sit up straight, get your pens or pencils ready, and let's glean some fun!

1. What was the name of Ruth's first husband (aka Naomi's son)?
   a. Mahlon
   b. Elimelech
   c. Kilion
   d. Babe

2. In Bethlehem, Naomi told her friends to no longer call her Naomi, which means pleasant, but Mara, which means *what*?
   a. widow
   b. bitter
   c. woman without sons
   d. nasty

3. At the first meal Boaz shared with Ruth, he invited her to dunk her bread in *what*?
   a. coffee
   b. milk
   c. olive oil
   d. wine vinegar

4. Boaz was Naomi and Ruth's *what*?
   a. second cousin once removed
   b. poor uncle
   c. guardian-redeemer
   d. field foreman

5. On her first day in the field, Ruth gleaned *what*?
   a. blisters
   b. barley
   c. wheat
   d. wisdom

6. After falling asleep on the threshing floor, Boaz woke up to find *what*?
    a. Ruth lying at his feet
    b. Naomi washing the floor
    c. Rats eating the grain
    d. Moabites knocking at the door

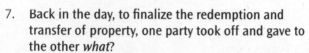

7. Back in the day, to finalize the redemption and transfer of property, one party took off and gave to the other *what*?
    a. his signet ring
    b. his robe
    c. his sandal
    d. his mantle

8. When Ruth gave birth to her son, the women told Naomi that her daughter-in-law was better to her than *what*?
    a. much gold
    b. many cattle
    c. a husband
    d. seven sons

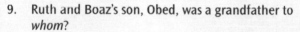

9. Ruth and Boaz's son, Obed, was a grandfather to *whom*?
    a. Jesse
    b. Solomon
    c. David
    d. Diah

Quiz 14—Wrap-up

Well, I hope you liked all that family history. It's amazing what happens when we decide to stick close to our loved ones, follow the Lord, and never look back. May you resolve to do the same.

> *"Don't urge me to leave you or to turn back from you. Where you go I will go, and where you stay I will stay. Your people will be my people and your God my God."*
> RUTH 1:16–17 NIV

Quiz 15

Welcome to quiz 15. They call me Eli. I was a priest and a judge of Israel before the time of kings. You can find most of my story in the beginning of 1 Samuel. Although I did well in my professional life, I had a lot to learn about how to raise a family. But I'll let *you* be the judge as you try to answer the next nine questions.

1. Eli had two sons named *what*?
   a. Wallach and Whitney
   b. Hophni and Phinehas
   c. Abinadab and Jesse
   d. Shammah and Eliab

2. The temple in which Eli served was *where*?
   a. Ramah   c. Bethel
   b. Philadelphia   d. Shiloh

3. When Eli overheard Hannah's prayer for a son, he thought she was *what*?
   a. a prophetess
   b. expectant
   c. a wine imbiber
   d. presumptuous

4. Eli's sons were considered "wicked" because they *what*?
   a. treated the offering of the Lord with contempt
   b. were always drunk
   c. committed adultery
   d. tried to kidnap Toto

5. Because Eli honored his sons more than God, the Lord said all but which one of the following would happen?
   a. None of Eli's male descendents would live to an old age.
   b. Eli's sons would die on the same day.
   c. Eli's grandson would become a traitor to Israel.
   d. The Lord's altar would grieve Eli's heart.

6. When young Samuel experienced his first prophecy, Eli was *what*?
   a. deaf
   b. almost blind
   c. asleep
   d. inventing the cotton gin

7. When Eli found out that both his sons had been killed and the ark captured, he *what*?
   a. tore his clothes
   b. had an "ark" attack
   c. mourned for forty days
   d. fell and broke his neck

8. When Eli's pregnant daughter-in-law found out that both her husband and father-in-law had died, she gave birth to *whom*?
   a. Eekami, which means "born in pain"
   b. Ben-Oni, which means "son of my sorrow"
   c. Ichabod, which means "inglorious"
   d. Beriah, which means "tragedy"

9. To fulfill the word of the Lord, the king who removed Abiathar, a descendant of Eli, from serving as a priest was *who*?
   a. Saul
   b. Solomon
   c. David
   d. Nat

Quiz 15—Wrap-up

As you can see, I put more effort into judging Israel for forty years than I did in raising my sons to be godly men. But that's water under the bridge, and right now, I see Samuel—one whom I *didn't* fail—standing in the wings, ready to launch you into the next quiz. God bless!

> *If [church officials] don't know*
> *how to control their own families,*
> *how can they look after God's people?*
> 1 TIMOTHY 3:5 CEV

Quiz 16

How prophetic that we meet here—you and me, Samuel the judge, prophet, and priest. This quiz will test how well you know Israel's history before and after the first and second kings. So let's get started.

1. What was the name of Samuel's father?
   a. Jeroham
   b. Elihu
   c. Mr. Adams
   d. Elkanah

2. In what god's house did the Philistines store the ark of the Lord?
   a. Ashtoreth
   b. Baal
   c. Chemosh
   d. Dagon

3. After their god was decapitated, the Philistines sent away the ark of the Lord, filled with five golden *what*?
   a. fleeces
   b. heads of state
   c. rats and tumors
   d. sovereigns

4. Samuel was a circuit judge, traveling to different places but always returning to his home in *where*?
   a. Bethel
   b. Gigal
   c. Ramah
   d. Adamsville

5. Samuel's sons did not walk in their father's footsteps. What were their names?
   a. Joel and Abijah
   b. Jason and Argonaut
   c. Ebenezer and Mizpah
   d. Nahash and Jabesh

6. When he first met Samuel, Saul was in search of *what*?
   a. Philistines
   b. donkeys
   c. his alter ego, Paul
   d. God

7. Following a victorious battle, Samuel set up an earthy memorial called Ebenezer, which means *what*?
   a. Flint of Skin
   b. Rock of Praises
   c. Boulder of Battle
   d. Stone of Help

8. To King Agag of the Amalekites, Samuel did *what*?

   a. put "a gag" over his mouth
   b. scorned him
   c. hacked him up
   d. hid him

9. Samuel's final meeting with Saul was at the home of a medium *where*?
   a. Gath
   b. Endor
   c. Witchita
   d. Mizpah

Quiz 16—Wrap-up

So there you have it! I hope you enjoyed your time with me. Before you go on to the next quiz, I leave you with this bit of wisdom: With all your might, remain faithful to God, not men.

"Only fear the LORD, and serve Him in truth with all your heart; for consider what great things He has done for you."
1 SAMUEL 12:24 NKJV

Quiz 17

Hear ye, hear ye! All rise for the first God-appointed king of Israel! My name is Saul, a ruler, music lover, and mighty soldier who started out fairly well but had a lousy finish. But let's not harp on it. Instead, take a seat as we test your knowledge of my life in this next quiz.

1. Saul was from the tribe of *what*?
   a. Kishentell
   b. Judah
   c. Benjamin
   d. Ephraim

2. Immediately after Saul was anointed king of Israel, he began doing *what*?
   a. ruling
   b. fighting enemies
   c. prophesying
   d. raising taxes

3. The most outstanding feature of the new king Saul was *what*?
   a. his good looks
   b. that he was Kish's son
   c. his humility
   d. his stature

4. What was the name of Saul's cousin, who was also commander of his army?
   a. Abner
   b. Joab
   c. Abiel
   d. Patton

5. The Lord regretted making Saul king because Saul did *what*?
   a. overtaxed the people
   b. disobeyed the Lord
   c. tried to kill David
   d. sought a rare medium

6. Saul's daughter Merab should have been given to David to marry, but Saul gave her to *whom*?
   a. Ahimelech the Hittite
   b. Doeg the Edomite
   c. Adriel the Meholathite
   d. Homer the Brave

7. Saul told David he could have Princess Michal's hand in exchange for *what*?
   a. Goliath's sword
   b. 100 Philistine foreskins
   c. a chest of gold
   d. Ahimelech's head

8. The second time David spared Saul's life, instead of killing him, David did *what*?

   a. tore off a piece of Saul's robe
   b. broke Saul's harp in two
   c. kidnapped Saul's daughter
   d. stole Saul's spear and water

9. After the Philistines found Saul slain, they did *what*?
   a. put his head on a post
   b. sent his body home on a cart
   c. fastened his corpse to a wall and his head in the temple
   d. cremated his remains

Quiz 17—Wrap-up

Well, if you weren't too familiar with my story before, perhaps you are now. I hope you had some fun with this quiz and gleaned some insight as to how *not* to live your life. Oh, if only I'd been more faithful to the Lord! But enough about me. Goliath, a giant of a man, is up next. And I wish you success with his quiz!

> *"The LORD has sought out a man after his own heart and appointed him ruler of his people, because you have not kept the LORD's command."*
> 1 SAMUEL 13:14 NIV

Quiz 18

Grrrrr. So, you think you can answer some questions about me—the great Goliath—and my battle with that scrawny shepherd boy David, huh? Think you're that smart, do you? Well, let's just see! I'm ready when you are.

1. Goliath confronted David *where*?
    a. at the Giant store
    b. in the Valley of Elah
    c. on Mount Ararat
    d. in the Valley of Siddim

2. Goliath was over how many feet tall?
    a. seven
    b. eight
    c. nine
    d. ten

3. Goliath was from *where*?

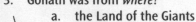

    a. the Land of the Giants
    b. Ashdod
    c. Ekron
    d. Gath

4. How many days did Goliath taunt the armies of Israel?
    a. seven
    b. fourteen
    c. thirty
    d. forty

5. Goliath asked David, "Am I a dog, that you come at me with" *what*?
    a. "your bones"
    b. "sticks"
    c. "a collar"
    d. "stones"

6. In delivering the final and fatal blow to Goliath, David used *what*?
   a. a stone
   b. a sword
   c. a spear
   d. a javelin

7. What did David do with Goliath's head?
   a. buried it
   b. tacked it to a Philistine wall
   c. mounted it in his den
   d. brought it to Jerusalem

8. Ahimelech of Nob stored Goliath's sword *where*?

   a. at the Men's Big and Tall armory
   b. with the Urim and the Thummim
   c. behind the ephod
   d. amid the showbread

9. In another battle with the Philistines, Goliath's brother was killed. What was his name?
   a. Lahmi
   b. Achish
   c. Maoch
   d. Broliath

Quiz 18—Wrap-up

If you did well with this quiz, then I guess you're the new champion. But I'm not going to lose my head in congratulating you. I'm just not that friendly a guy. But Jonathan, the next person you will meet, is. Meanwhile, I leave you with what little wisdom I—a thick-headed giant—gleaned from my battle with David:

> *"The LORD does not deliver by sword or by spear; for the battle is the LORD's."*
> 1 SAMUEL 17:47 NASB

Quiz 19

Hail to Prince Jonathan—that's me! My dad is Saul, a man in whose footsteps I *definitely* did not walk. But you probably know my story—or perhaps you don't! There's only one way to find out. Put on your thinking cap and begin with question 1.

1. What was Jonathan's mother's name?
   a. Ahinoam
   b. Queenie
   c. Cozbi
   d. Dinah

2. Jonathan once disobeyed his father's rash order by doing *what*?
   a. scratching
   b. eating honey
   c. killing twenty Philistines
   d. deserting the army

3. Which of the following did Jonathan *not* give to David?
   a. his robe and tunic
   b. his sword
   c. his bow and belt
   d. his shield

4. Indicating that David's life was in danger, Jonathan shot arrows near the stone of *what*?
   a. Rosetta
   b. Ezel
   c. Zoheleth
   d. Ebenezer

5. The ill-fated messenger who informed David of Jonathan's and Saul's deaths was *what*?
   a. Saul's armor bearer
   b. an Amalekite
   c. a Philistine
   d. Western Union

6. *The Song of the Bow*—David's lament over the deaths of Saul and Jonathan—was recorded *where*?
   a. Book of Jashar
   b. Abbey Road Studios
   c. Book of David
   d. Book of the Covenant

7. Jonathan, his brothers, and Saul died *where*?
   a. Mount Horeb
   b. Mount Gilboa
   c. Mount Ebal
   d. Mount Enattack

8. When he was told his father, Jonathan, was killed, Mephibosheth was how old?
   a. two years
   b. three years
   c. four years
   d. five years

9. Mephibosheth claimed his servant betrayed him. What was this servant's name?
   a. Hazael
   b. Godfrey
   c. Ziba
   d. Zela

Quiz 19—Wrap-up

So, that's my story—and more! Hope you enjoyed your time with me. David, my good friend, is coming up to quiz you next. So, I leave you with this blessing:

For my brethren and companions' sakes,
I will now say, Peace be within thee.
PSALM 122:8 KJV

Quiz 20

Hello. It's me, David—you know, the man after God's own heart. I've been waiting for you! As you probably know, my life was anything but dull. So I'm sure you are going to enjoy our time together. Are you ready for some really great quizzing? If so, let's go!

1. The name of David's father was *what*?
   a. Mogen
   b. Jesse
   c. Eliab
   d. Judah

2. To whom did Saul give David's wife Michal to wed?
   a. Paltiel
   b. Laish
   c. Adriel
   d. Nesmith

3. David committed adultery with Bathsheba, the wife of Uriah the *what*?

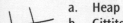

   a. Heap
   b. Gittite
   c. Hittite
   d. Edomite

4. In front of Achish the king of Gath, David pretended to be *what*?
   a. infested with fleas
   b. wounded
   c. an enemy of Saul
   d. insane

5. David married Abigail, the widow of Nabal, whose name means *what*?
   a. stone-hearted
   b. fool
   c. apoplectic
   d. stingy

6. The name of David's firstborn son was *what*?
    a. Amnon
    b. Absalom
    c. Adonijah
    d. Solomon

7. Michal was displeased with her husband, David, because he *what*?
    a. was a royal pain
    b. committed adultery
    c. publicly disrobed
    d. danced in front of the ark

8. When David and his men were starving, they ate *what*?

    a. Hungry-Man Dinners
    b. grain on the Sabbath
    c. Nabal's sheep
    d. consecrated bread

9. On his deathbed, David instructed Solomon to show what kindness to the sons of Barzillai the Gileadite?
    a. give them a place at the king's table
    b. make them part of the mighty men
    c. move them up a few "barz" on the social ladder
    d. increase their wealth

Quiz 20—Wrap-up

Well, that about wraps things up. I hope you finished well.
I wish you success as you move forward to the next quiz,
with Nathan the prophet. And remember, always go with
God!

*David continued to succeed in everything
he did, for the LORD was with him.*
1 SAMUEL 18:14 NLT

Quiz 21

I *knew* we'd meet up eventually. After all, I, Nathan, *am* a prophet! And I've "seen" some things that would make your head spin. Perhaps you're familiar with some of them. Ready to find out? Good, because here we go!

1. After receiving a vision from God, Nathan told David *what*?
    a. David's son's throne would be established forever.
    b. David should build God's house.
    c. David should attack the Philistines.
    d. David would never be a letterman.

2. In Nathan's parable to David, Bathsheba was metaphorically described as *what*?
    a. a tub of Imperial margarine
    b. a harlot
    c. a little ewe lamb
    d. fool's gold

3. After Nathan confronted David about the shepherd king's adultery with Bathsheba and murder of Uriah, David said *what*?
    a. "I feel sheepish."
    b. "May the LORD withhold His hand from me."
    c. "Please spare my life."
    d. "I have sinned against the LORD."

4. After Nathan predicted the death of David and Bathsheba's firstborn son, the child fell ill and then died within how many days?
    a. three
    b. seven
    c. thirty
    d. forty

5. The Lord sent Nathan to rename Bathsheba's son Solomon *what*?
   a. Tubheba
   b. Jedidiah
   c. Jethro
   d. Ishbosheth

6. David instructed Nathan and what priest to anoint Solomon king?
   a. Flanagan
   b. Zadok
   c. Abiathar
   d. Ahimelech

7. A contemporary of Nathan's, Benaiah was one of David's *what*?

   a. uncles
   b. priests
   c. messengers
   d. mighty men

8. How did Nathan escort Solomon, as the soon-to-be-king, to his coronation?
   a. in a Buick Regal
   b. in the king's chariot
   c. on the king's mule
   d. on the royal stallion

9. After Solomon's anointing by the priests, the people played *what*?
   a. cards
   b. flutes
   c. trumpets
   d. tambourines

Quiz 21—Wrap-up

Well, I predicted a great finish for you! Was I right? I hope so. Now I've got to run. I'm on the King's business, don't you know. But I leave you in the hands of your next host, Absalom—the man who prized the kingship. So good-bye for now!

Irresponsible talk makes a real mess of things,
but a reliable reporter is a healing presence.
PROVERBS 13:17 MSG

Quiz 22

Oh, I'm sorry. I didn't know you were here. I was too busy blow-drying my beautiful hair. Always want to look my best. They call me Absalom, and as you can see, I'm very handsome—a number 10 from the top of my head to the soles of my feet. So, I guess you're ready for this quiz. Let me set my comb down, and we'll brush up on my life story.

1. Absalom was the son of King David and *who*?
   a. Narcissa
   b. Abigail
   c. Maacah
   d. Haggith

2. Amnon, Absalom's half brother, raped Absalom's sister, who was named *what*?
   a. Tamar
   b. Dinah
   c. Chloe
   d. Deborah

3. After murdering Amnon, Absalom fled to Geshur until *what*?
   a. his father's anger abated
   b. three years had passed
   c. Tamar pleaded for him to return home
   d. he was named the "hair" apparent

4. At the end of every year, Absalom would cut his mane, which weighed about how much?
   a. eight ounces
   b. two hundred shekels
   c. eighty talents
   d. a hair over six pounds

5. To obtain a meeting with the elusive Joab, Absalom did *what*?
   a. scheduled an appointment with Joab's secretary
   b. asked King David to intercede
   c. rode his chariot to Joab's house
   d. set Joab's field on fire

6. While leading his rebellion against King David, Absalom followed the advice of *whom*?
    a. Dear Abby
    b. Ahithophel
    c. Hushai
    d. Abiathar

7. As Absalom rode his mule into battle, what part of his person got caught in a tree?
    a. a lower limb
    b. his head
    c. his mantle
    d. his armor

8. Who stabbed Absalom in the heart?

    a. Joab
    b. Abner
    c. Jonathan
    d. Cupid

9. Upon hearing of his son Absalom's death, David did *what*?
    a. cried, "O Absalom, my son, my son!"
    b. celebrated at the city gates
    c. mourned for forty days and nights
    d. had the ark returned to Jerusalem

Quiz 22—Wrap-up

So, that's my story. Not a very pleasant one, I fear. But I guess I let my passion for power really go to my head. Hopefully you've learned something and won't get caught making the same mistakes I did. Before you head out to meet with Solomon, here's a little proverb to think about:

His own iniquities entrap the wicked man,
and he is caught in the cords of his sin.
PROVERBS 5:22 NKJV

Quiz 23

Well, you, like me—Solomon—are very wise, for you are testing your knowledge of the Good Book. How are you faring so far? Well, I hope! Now you'll have the opportunity to see how much you know about me. Let us begin at the beginning.

1. Solomon, the son of King David and Bathsheba, was born *where*?
    a. Hebron
    b. Jerusalem
    c. Gaza
    d. Bethel

2. After presuming to be king, Adonijah, in fear of Solomon, ran and took hold of the horns of *what*?
    a. the bulls of Pamplona
    b. the shofar
    c. the altar
    d. the Most Holy Place

3. After asking God for a discerning heart, Solomon received wisdom as well as *what*?

    a. women and riches
    b. riches and honor
    c. honor and glory
    d. glory and power

4. When preparing to build the temple, Solomon requested cedar and pine from *whom*?
    a. Homer of Depot
    b. Hermon of Sidon
    c. Ben of Hur
    d. Hiram of Tyre

5. Solomon's home was called *what*?
    a. The Sol Mahal
    b. Palace of the Forest of Lebanon
    c. Hall of Pillars
    d. Colonnade of Conquest

6. Every year, merchant ships brought Solomon gold, silver, ivory, apes, and *what*?
    a. bananas
    b. horses
    c. parrots
    d. baboons

7. In Psalm 127:1, Solomon wrote, "Unless the LORD builds the house, its builders" *what*?
    a. "work without accident insurance"
    b. "build on the sand"
    c. "labor in vain"
    d. "toil with weakness"

8. In the King James Bible, the phrase "vanity" and *what* appears seven times in the book of Ecclesiastes?

    a. "vexation of spirit"
    b. "fair"
    c. "a sore travail"
    d. "grasping at the wind"

9. In Song of Solomon, the king's young bride is referred to as *whom*?
    a. Bridezilla
    b. Sheba
    c. pharaoh's daughter
    d. the Shulammite

Quiz 23—Wrap-up

Well, as you probably know, I started out on the right path
with God but ended up turning down the wrong road.
And, as my legacy, I ended up bequeathing an overtaxed
kingdom to a man named Rehoboam, whom you'll meet
in the next section. Oh, if only I'd kept my feet on the right
path. It's too late for me but not for you. Just remember
to:

Trust in the Lord with all your heart
and lean not on your own understanding;
in all your ways submit to him,
and he will make your paths straight.
PROVERBS 3:5–6 NIV

Quiz 24

Hi! Rehoboam, here. I, the last king of the united Israel, made some split decisions, much to the demise of the whole nation. But you probably already knew that, right? Well, maybe not. So, let's proceed with this quiz and see how much you really *do* know!

1. Rehoboam was the son of Naamah and *whom*?
    a. Naapah
    b. Absalom
    c. Solomon
    d. Adonijah

2. Rehoboam was crowned king *where*?
    a. Shechem
    b. Jerusalem
    c. Coronado
    d. Hebron

3. How old was Rehoboam when he became king?

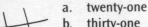

    a. twenty-one
    b. thirty-one
    c. forty-one
    d. fifty-one

4. The "heavy yoke" that Rehoboam laid upon the people was *what*?
    a. a five-pound ostrich egg
    b. taxes and conscription of labor
    c. worship of foreign gods
    d. restrictive laws

5. What servant of Rehoboam was stoned to death by the people?
    a. Levy
    b. Nebat
    c. Adoniram
    d. Zabad

6. When the nation divided, Rehoboam became the ruler of two tribes named *what*?
    a. Judah and Benjamin
    b. Apache and Mohawk
    c. Reuben and Ephraim
    d. Gad and Joseph

7. To keep his people from the Jerusalem temple, Jeroboam, king of the remaining ten tribes, made them worship *what*?
    a. American idols
    b. two golden calves
    c. Molech
    d. Baal

8. The granddaughter of Absalom and the wife who Rehoboam loved most was named *what*?

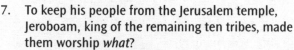

    a. Ab-salami
    b. Mahalath
    c. Maakah
    d. Abihail

9. When the evil Rehoboam died, what prince ruled in his place?
    a. Charming
    b. Attai
    c. Ziza
    d. Abijah

Quiz 24—Wrap-up

Well, I seemed to make some stormy decisions that resulted in a heavy reign. What I should have done was heed wise—instead of foolish—counsel and treat my people with kindness. Before I leave you in the hands of your next guide, Jehoshaphat, I pray you heed the following adage:

A wise man will hear and increase in learning, and a man of understanding will acquire wise counsel.
PROVERBS 1:5 NASB

Quiz 25

Well, leaping lizards, you've finally arrived. I, Jehoshaphat, am jumping up and down for joy! It's good to see your face. As you may already know, I was once king of Judah. Better than that—I was an ancestor of Christ! My story begins in 1 Kings 15:24. Let's start our quiz there!

1. Jehoshaphat's father (whose name rhymes with the Spanish word for "table") was *who*?
    a. Jehoshathin
    b. Asa
    c. Baasha
    d. Nadab

2. The infamous king who ruled Israel during the seventeenth year of Jehoshaphat's reign was *who*?
    a. Nebat
    b. Evelknievel
    c. Jerobaom
    d. Ahab

3. When Moabites, Ammonites, and Meunites came to battle Jehoshaphat, what did he proclaim throughout Judah?
    a. a call to arms
    b. a retreat
    c. a fast
    d. a sacrifice

4. The priest Jahaziel told Judah, "The battle is" *what*?
    a. "feudal"
    b. "not yours, but God's"
    c. "yours to win"
    d. "for the mighty men of valor to fight"

5. The front line of Jehoshaphat's army was comprised of *what*?
    a. singers
    b. charioteers
    c. archers
    d. sitting ducks

6. The enemy armies ended up *what*?
   a. retreating
   b. being swallowed by the earth
   c. destroying each other
   d. surrendering

7. After a terrific victory, Jehoshaphat and his people celebrated in the Lord in the valley of Berachah, which means *what*?
   a. Berachfast of Champions
   b. Victory
   c. Triumph of God
   d. Praise

8. How many years did Jehoshaphat reign in Jerusalem?
   a. fifteen
   b. twenty
   c. twenty-five
   d. thirty

9. Jehoshaphat's son, the next king, was named *what*?
   a. Jehoram
   b. Reiner
   c. Azariah
   d. Michael

Quiz 25—Wrap-up

So, that's my story. I'll admit, I did stray from the Lord, a time or two, but I think He was pleased with me because my heart was definitely in the right place—secure with Him. If you stand with God, nothing can stop you.

> *"Believe in the LORD your God,*
> *and you will be able to stand firm. Believe*
> *in his prophets, and you will succeed."*
> 2 CHRONICLES 20:20 NLT

Quiz 26

So you think you know your Bible stories, eh? Well, I (Ahab) and my wife, Jezebel, would like to challenge you. You know, find your weak spots. Are you man or woman enough to test your knowledge? Do you dare? If so, let's go!

1. Ahab, King of Israel, should not be confused with another Ahab, son of Kolaiah, who, according to Jeremiah 29:21–22, met his demise *how*?
   a. shot by an arrow
   b. hung by the Philistines
   c. riveted by frogs
   d. burned by the king of Babylon

2. Jezebel promoted the worship of *what*?
   a. Baal
   b. Molech
   c. Chemosh
   d. Idulla trees

3. The prophet who was constantly bringing Ahab negative reports was named *what*?

   a. Baad News Bearra
   b. Elisha
   c. Nathan
   d. Elijah

4. Ahab made a treaty with the king of Syria, named Ben-*what*?
   a. en Jerry
   b. Ammi
   c. Hadad
   d. Hur

5. Ahab coveted Naboth's *what*?
   a. wife
   b. riches
   c. vineyard
   d. ships

6. While in his chariot during a battle, how was Ahab killed?
   a. by a whale harpoon
   b. by an arrow
   c. by stampeding horses
   d. in a chariot collision

7. When Ahab's chariot was being washed by a pool, "the dogs licked up his blood" while *what*?
   a. "the prostitutes bathed"
   b. "his servants checked the oil"
   c. "Ishmael praised"
   d. "Jezebel mourned"

8. When Jezebel heard Jehu had come to Israel, she "painted her eyes" and *what*?
   a. "bedecked herself in jewels"
   b. "gave her nails a second coat"
   c. "arranged her hair"
   d. "changed her dress"

9. In meeting her demise, Jezebel was thrown out a window then *what*?
   a. stoned by harlots
   b. trampled by horses
   c. drown in a pool
   d. stabbed by Jehu

Quiz 26—Wrap-up

Well, I guess you have some idea why we were so wicked.
We totally turned away from the Lord and literally went
to the dogs. In Revelation 2:20, Jezebel's name is used as
a prime example of extreme evil, giving you some idea of
whom we served. What do you do when the wicked flare?

> *Do not let yourself be overcome by evil,*
> *but overcome (master) evil with good.*
> ROMANS 12:21 AMP

Quiz 27

Welcome! I envisioned us meeting. Elijah here! I was God's prophet and saw many amazing things. I also accomplished some fantastic feats. Let's see how much you know about me. Pencils ready? Let's get ready to make our mark!

1. By the Brook Kerith, Elijah *what*?
    a. propheted nicely
    b. brought down fire from the Lord
    c. was fed by ravens
    d. thirsted for God

2. Elijah physically revived the widow's son by *what*?
    a. breathing on him
    b. thrice stretching himself out on the boy
    c. doing the Himmel-ich maneuver
    d. anointing him with oil

3. The servant who was afraid to tell Ahab that he'd found Elijah was named *what*?
    a. Jeeves
    b. Asaiah
    c. Jarha
    d. Obadiah

4. Elijah executed the prophets of Baal *where*?
    a. the brook Kishon
    b. the brook Zered
    c. the brook Noevil
    d. the brook Kidron

5. After Elijah slept under a broom tree, an angel told him "Get up and eat" because *what*?
    a. "you'll need your strength"
    b. "breakfast is the most important meal of the day"
    c. "the journey is too much for you"
    d. "you must rest forty days and nights"

6. When Elijah met Elisha, what was the latter doing?
    a. transcendental meditation
    b. fishing
    c. walking down the road
    d. plowing

7. Who did God tell Elijah to anoint as king over Syria?
    a. Regis Philbin
    b. Hazael
    c. Rezin
    d. Hezion

8. Elijah was taken up to heaven in a weather anomaly known as a *what*?
    a. whirlwind
    b. thunder bolt
    c. waterspout
    d. tsunami

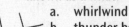
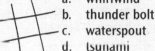

9. Before Elijah went up into heaven, what did Elisha ask him for?
    a. his forwarding address
    b. his chariot
    c. a double portion of his spirit
    d. his miracle-working powers

Quiz 27—Wrap-up

To really hear God you have to know *how* to listen. Have you heard His voice lately? Are your ears open? Elisha's were. And I predict he'll be coming up soon. Watch for him.

> *And after the earthquake a fire; but the LORD*
> *was not in the fire: and after the fire*
> *a still small voice. And. . .Elijah heard it.*
> 1 KINGS 19:12–13 KJV

Quiz 28

Greetings from Israel! My name is Jehu, and I'm an army commander who became a king. Boy, the stories I could tell you! What a life I led! I was bold but made quite a few mistakes. Anyway, I will be guiding you through this next quiz. Since my story starts in 1 Kings 19:16, we'll begin there. Ready or not, here we go!

1. Jehu was to kill whoever escaped the sword of *whom*?
   a. Hazael, king of Syria
   b. Ahab, king of Israel
   c. Inigo Montoya of *Princess Bride*
   d. Ben-Hadad, king of Syria

2. In retribution for Ahab's thievery, Jehu killed Ahab's ancestor, Joram, and had him buried *where*?
   a. wilderness of Sin
   b. valley of Achor
   c. the field of Naboth the Jezreelite
   d. Mount Hor

3. When Jehu assassinated Joram, where was the latter seated?
   a. in a balcony seat at Ford's Theater
   b. on his throne
   c. at a table
   d. in a chariot

4. What was the name of Jehu's captain?
   a. James T. Kirk
   b. Bidkar
   c. Heman
   d. Pekah

5. Immediately after Jehu assassinated Joram, he mortally wounded *who*?
   a. Ahaziah
   b. Jezebel
   c. Jehonadab
   d. Attila

6. When Jezebel greeted Jehu, she called him a Zimri (2 Kings 9:31), referring to a *what*?
   a. seven-day reign
   b. traitor who'd killed a king to seize the throne
   c. white lion
   d. king of Magog

7. The heads of Ahab's seventy sons were *what*?
   a. de-crowned
   b. shaved
   c. eternally parted
   d. put in baskets

8. What did Jehu invite the worshippers of Baal to?
   a. a Baal-room dance
   b. a great sacrifice
   c. a bounteous feast
   d. a grand party

9. Although Jehu razed the temple of Baal, what did he *not* do?
   a. raze the bar
   b. destroy the sacred pillar of Baal
   c. keep people from sacrificing their children
   d. turn from worshipping golden calves

Quiz 28—Wrap-up

I know, I know. I fell short of God's expectations. I didn't
give Him my whole heart. Have you given God *all* of yours?
If so, you will be blessed. If not, why not do so today?

*So love the Lord your God with
all your heart, soul, and strength.*
DEUTERONOMY 6:5 CEV

Quiz 29

How prophetic that we meet here—just as I envisioned.
My name is Elisha. I come after Elijah, alphabetically and
chronologically. Perhaps you are familiar with my life story
and all the miracles I've performed. Want to see *how* familiar?
Great! Let's raise those pencils and get cracking!

1. After Elijah was taken up to heaven, what did Elisha do?
   a. He fled in a chariot.
   b. He parted the Jordan.
   c. He fell to the ground.
   d. He dismantled Elijah's staff.

2. After some youths mocked the bald-headed Elisha, they were *what*?
   a. eaten by lions
   b. bitten by scorpions
   c. mauled by two she-bears
   d. struck with receding hairlines

3. To keep a widow's sons from slavery due to debt, Elisha multiplied her *what*?

   a. oil
   b. talents
   c. crops
   d. tables

4. What did Elisha heal Naaman of?
   a. Marcus
   b. a withered foot
   c. leprosy
   d. boils

5. Naaman worshipped at the temple of *what*?
   a. Rimmon
   b. Baal
   c. Chemosh
   d. Doom

6. Elisha's devious servant was named *what*?
    a. Hobson
    b. Gehazi
    c. Ziba
    d. Zimri

7. Coming to the aid of the sons of the prophets, Elisha made *what* float?
    a. hope
    b. a bronze candleholder
    c. a silver basin
    d. an ax head

8. After Elisha's prayer, what did God strike the Syrian army with?

    a. lightning
    b. blindness
    c. dysentery
    d. Spam—a lot!

9. The last miracle connected with Elisha happened *where*?
    a. in the Valley of Elah
    b. on the banks of the Jordan
    c. in his grave
    d. on the Hudson

Quiz 29—Wrap-up

My life was miraculous. But it was all due to the power of God. And what an awesome God He is! What a wonderful God we serve! Praise Him, praise Him!

> *Praise him for his acts of power;*
> *praise him for his surpassing greatness.*
> PSALM 150:2 NIV

Quiz 30

Hey! Joash here! I was a king who, like many before me, started out well but ended poorly. But you probably know at least part of my story. After all, my life is an open book (see 2 Kings and 2 Chronicles). I hope you know a little bit about me, because you'll need that knowledge to do well with this quiz. Are you prepared? Let's begin.

1. King Ahaziah's mother, who destroyed all the royal heirs, was named *what*?
   a. Jezebel
   b. Athaliah
   c. Zibiah
   d. Heirrazer

2. Ahaziah's son Joash was saved by Jehosheba, who was his *what*?
   a. nurse
   b. sister
   c. aunt
   d. hairy godmother

3. When Joash was hailed as king, what did his grandmother yell?
   a. "I'll get you, my pretty!"
   b. "Long live the king!"
   c. "Seize him! Seize him!"
   d. "Treason! Treason!"

4. How old was Joash when he was crowned king?
   a. six years old
   b. seven years old
   c. eight years old
   d. nine years old

5. On Joash's coronation day, what priest of Baal was killed at the altar?
   a. Baal-Zebub
   b. Zadok
   c. Mattan
   d. Korah

6. Joash's Uncle Jehoiada, the priest, took a chest and did *what*?
    a. stole the money inside
    b. bored a hole in its lid
    c. filled it with gold
    d. checked for a heartbeat

7. When Jehoiada died, he was *what*?
    a. leprous
    b. 130 years old
    c. a eunuch
    d. canonized

8. Joash commanded his cousin Zechariah be *what*?
    a. ex-communicated
    b. killed with the sword
    c. sold for "prophet"
    d. stoned to death

9. Joash's servants killed him while he *what*?
    a. lay in bed
    b. rode in his chariot
    c. sat on his throne
    d. lowered their wages

Quiz 30—Wrap-up

As you can see, after Jehoiada died and I lost his counsel, I made some rotten decisions. And they made for a bad end. Do you have someone who can give you good guidance? Remember:

*As iron sharpens iron,
so a friend sharpens a friend.*
PROVERBS 27:17 NLT

Quiz 31

Ready for the thirteenth king of Judah? Great! Because here I am. My name is Hezekiah. I was a major reformer who trusted in the God of Israel. Want to see how much you know about me? Great! I'm ready if you are! Let's launch right into things, shall we?

1. When Hezekiah became king, he destroyed Moses'
   bronze snake, which the people had called *what*?

   a. Asp-aragus
   b. Nehushtan
   c. Ophidia
   d. he who heals

2. When Hezekiah heard Sennacherib's boasts against
   the Lord, he tore his clothes and *what*?
   a. rubbed himself with ash
   b. rented his rooms
   c. covered himself with sackcloth
   d. sent for the prophet Amoz

3. After Hezekiah prayed to the Lord, what killed the
   Assyrian armies?
   a. trench mouth
   b. Eliakim
   c. fire
   d. the angel of the Lord

4. Sennacherib was killed while worshipping at the
   temple of the god named *what*?
   a. Nisroch
   b. Molech
   c. Chemosh
   d. Baal

5. What was copied during Hezekiah's reign?
   a. books of Xerox
   b. proverbs of Solomon
   c. books of Iddo the seer
   d. records of Nathan the prophet

6. When Hezekiah was suffering from a boil, Isaiah's remedy was *what*?
   a. to take two aspirins and call him in the morning
   b. to apply figs to the sore
   c. to dip his body in the Jordan
   d. to rub the boil with oil

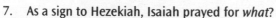

7. As a sign to Hezekiah, Isaiah prayed for *what*?
   a. the sun to stand still
   b. a vision of chariots of fire
   c. the shadow to go backward ten steps
   d. the moon to block the sun

8. Hezekiah made a mistake when he showed the temple treasures to *whom*?
   a. the Faux Pasians
   b. leaders of Syria
   c. the Philistines
   d. the delegates from Babylon

9. Hezekiah built a tunnel that *what*?
   a. brought water into the city
   b. allowed sewage to leave the city
   c. gave him special vision
   d. kept the golf course free of gophers

Quiz 31—Wrap-up

Well, as far as kings go, I was pretty loyal to the Lord our God. And because I walked in His ways, I was able to accomplish quite a few things, to His glory. Well, I've gotta go, but Ezra's coming up next to guide you through your next quiz. May God bless you!

Take delight in the LORD,
and he will give you the desires of your heart.
PSALM 37:4 NIV

Quiz 32

Hi, fellow student. Ezra here. I was a leader, a scribe, and a contemporary of Nehemiah, as well as a teacher, studier, and follower of God's word. Because I kept my focus on the Lord, I accomplished much. Let's see what *you* can achieve as you attempt to correctly answer the next nine questions.

1. The king of Persia who sent both Ezra and Nehemiah to Jerusalem was named *what*?
   a. Egress
   b. Artaxerxes
   c. Nebuchadnezzar
   d. Darius

2. At the canal of Ahava, Ezra proclaimed a fast and prayer for *what*?
   a. speed
   b. the temple
   c. riches
   d. protection

3. Hearing of the exiles' intermarriage with pagans, Ezra tore his clothes, plucked out some hair, and sat down *what*?

   a. appalled
   b. in ashes
   c. in pottery shards
   d. on a Cushian

4. The exiles confessed their improper marriages amid a *what*?
   a. drought
   b. dust storm
   c. tsunalimony
   d. heavy rain

5. Where did Ezra read the law to the people?
   a. at the Water Gate
   b. at the Horse Gate
   c. at the Sheep Gate
   d. at the Bill Gates

6. The exiles made and sat under booths, which they hadn't done since the days of *whom*?
    a. John of Wilkes
    b. Hezekiah of Judah
    c. Joash of Judah
    d. Joshua of Nun

7. In the court of the Persian king, Nehemiah was a *what*?
    a. baker
    b. cupbearer
    c. doormat
    d. captain

8. What Samarian governor was furious about the Jews rebuilding the wall?
    a. Sanballat the Horonite
    b. Tobiah the Ammonite
    c. Humpty the Dumpty
    d. Geshem the Arab

9. How long did it take to complete the wall?
    a. three weeks
    b. thirty-seven days
    c. seven weeks
    d. fifty-two days

Quiz 32—Wrap-up

Sometimes it takes a lot of courage to do the right thing.
Whenever you are faced with a hard decision, first pray,
and then be brave, and do as God leads you.

"Be of good courage, and do it."
EZRA **10:4** NKJV

Quiz 33

Welcome to Persia. That's where my story of romance, power, and intrigue takes place. My name is Esther, and you may be familiar with my tale. But let's see exactly how much you know, beginning with question 1.

1. King Xerxes ruled from his royal throne at the fortress of *where*?
   a. Solitude
   b. Asshur
   c. Nippur
   d. Susa

2. Who was King Xerxes's first wife?
   a. Duplitica
   b. Vashti
   c. Nitocris
   d. Zarei

3. Who was Esther's father?
   a. Mordecai
   b. Hadassah
   c. Mr. Williams
   d. Abihail

4. Haman did not like Mordecai because he wouldn't *what*?
   a. play reindeer games
   b. speak to him
   c. bow or pay homage to him
   d. attend to him

5. Hathach was the eunuch who *what*?
   a. attended Esther
   b. was in charge of the king's harem
   c. distributed the king's edict
   d. was a "unique" individual

6. What was Haman's wife's name?
   a. Zeresh
   b. Hormel
   c. Mehetabel
   d. Tirzah

7. The king took from Haman and gave to Mordecai *what*?
   a. a ration of Spam
   b. the royal scepter
   c. Haman's robe
   d. the king's signet ring

8. How many sons of Haman were hanged?

   a. seven
   b. eight
   c. nine
   d. ten

9. In celebration of God's deliverance, the Jews established a two-day festival called *what*?
   a. Hanukkah
   b. Purim
   c. Feast of Tabernacles
   d. Haman-eggs

Quiz 33—Wrap-up

Ever wonder why God brings certain situations into your life? Well, here's some good advice I received and now pass on to you:

> *Who knows but that you have come*
> *to the kingdom for such a time as this*
> *and for this very occasion?*
> ESTHER 4:14 AMP

Quiz 34

Bless my soul. There you are! Job here. My story is one of blessing, heartache, and blessing. Almost the whole world has heard my story of trial and triumph. But how much do they truly know? If you think you're up to snuff, let's test your memory with the following nine questions. Ready? Let's get started!

1. Where was Job from?
    a. U.S.
    b. Ur
    c. Ug
    d. Uz

2. In the beginning of his story, Job had *what*?
    a. employment
    b. seven sons and three daughters
    c. eight thousand sheep
    d. four thousand camels

3. Who stole Job's oxen and donkeys?

    a. Sabeans
    b. rustlers
    c. Chaldeans
    d. Edomites

4. What struck the corners of Job's eldest son's house?
    a. a wrecking ball
    b. hail
    c. lightning
    d. a mighty wind

5. After being struck with boils, Job scraped himself with *what*?
    a. sandpaper
    b. a boiler plate
    c. broken pottery
    d. his fingernails

6. Job's wife told him to *what*?
    a. "Rub ashes upon your skin."
    b. "Gather figs and make a poultice."
    c. "Seek advice from your friends."
    d. "Curse God and die."

7. What did God tell Job's friends to sacrifice?
    a. a fly
    b. seven bulls and ten rams
    c. seven bulls and seven rams
    d. ten bulls and ten rams

8. The Lord restored Job's losses when he *what*?
    a. repented in dust and ashes
    b. prayed for his friends
    c. forgave his wife
    d. was no longer boiling mad

9. After God's restoration, Job had more daughters, the eldest of whom was named *what*?
    a. Jemimah
    b. Employia
    c. Keziah
    d. Keren-Happuch

Quiz 34—Wrap-up

No matter what your problems or sorrows, take them to the Lord and know that He can do wonders in your life. Just keep walking that walk of faith, and keep your hope alive.

> *You have heard of Job's perseverance and have seen what the Lord finally brought about.*
> *The Lord is full of compassion and mercy.*
> JAMES 5:11 NIV

Quiz 35

Greetings from Jerusalem. My name is Isaiah. I was a scribe and a prophet. And parts of my book are quoted more than fifty times in the New Testament! Cool, huh? Are you ready to discover how much you know about me? If so, let's go!

1. Isaiah was the son of *whom*?
   a. Yousaiah
   b. Amoz
   c. Shear-Jashub
   d. Eleazar

2. Isaiah had his famous vision of the Lord on the throne during the last days of the king named *what*?
   a. Uzziah
   b. Jotham
   c. Martin Luther
   d. Hezekiah

3. In Isaiah's vision, the temple was filled with *what*?
   a. incensed angels
   b. cherubim
   c. seraphim
   d. the Lord's train

4. What did one of the angels touch Isaiah's lips with?
   a. tongs
   b. ChapStick
   c. a live coal
   d. his wings

5. In Isaiah 14, the term "morning star" refers to *what*?
   a. Matt Lauer
   b. Nebuchadnezzar
   c. Ahab
   d. Lucifer

6. In Isaiah 26:3, the prophet writes that he "whose mind is steadfast" will *what*?
    a. be a quick thinker
    b. have perfect peace
    c. abide in God
    d. be blessed

7. In Isaiah 45:1, Isaiah foretells God using as His instrument the Persian king named *what*?
    a. Cyrus
    b. Harpo
    c. Darius
    d. Ahasuerus

8. Twice Isaiah says, "There is no peace for" *whom*?
    a. "Babylon"
    b. "the faint of heart"
    c. "the jigsaw puzzle"
    d. "the wicked"

9. In Isaiah 62:4, the prophet predicts that the people and their city of Zion will someday be called *what*?
    a. Repairer and Restorer
    b. Shepherds and Fuller's Field
    c. Hephzibah and Beulah
    d. Eliakim and Hilkiah

Quiz 35—Wrap-up

I faced many dangers in my life, but I always had the
courage to speak my mind because I stayed close to God.
Stand on God's promises and you will not fall.

> *"Don't be afraid, for I am with you.*
> *Don't be discouraged, for I am your God.*
> *I will strengthen you and help you.*
> *I will hold you up with my victorious right hand."*
> ISAIAH 41:10 NLT

Quiz 36

Hello, and welcome! Jeremiah here. I was a prophet of the Old Testament, and I ministered during the reigns of the last five kings of Judah. Many opposed me, but I continued to carry God's message. God knows all about me. Do you? Let's find out.

1. Jeremiah is also known as *what*?
    a. a bullfrog
    b. the weeping prophet
    c. the naysayer
    d. the stricken

2. God called Jeremiah to be a prophet during the reign of which king of Judah?
    a. Hezekiah
    b. Jehoshaphat
    c. Josiah
    d. King James

3. Jeremiah wrote that above all things the heart is *what*?

    a. shattered
    b. deceitful
    c. vein
    d. sorrowful

4. In Jeremiah 18, the Lord told Jeremiah to go to the house of *whom*?
    a. Lords
    b. God
    c. Rahab
    d. the potter

5. What priest struck Jeremiah and then put him in stocks?
    a. Madoff
    b. Pashhur
    c. Immer
    d. Zephaniah

6. Jeremiah had a vision of two baskets of *what*?
   a. poesies
   b. barley
   c. figs
   d. wine bottles

7. What false prophet broke a yoke from Jeremiah's neck?
   a. Hananiah
   b. Balaam
   c. Ahijah
   d. Emeril

8. The group of men who would drink no wine were called *what*?

   a. Teetotalers
   b. Recabites
   c. Jonadabians
   d. Nomadites

9. Ebed-Melech the Cushite released Jeremiah from *what*?
   a. Lily's pad
   b. the stocks
   c. Babylon
   d. the dungeon

Quiz 36—Wrap-up

Well, as you can see, my life wasn't easy. But whose is
these days? Regardless of our fortune, we can always rely
on God and the power of His love to pull us out of the pits.
Your next guide, Ezekiel, can tell you more about courage.
So I'll leave you in his capable hands.

> *"I have loved you with an everlasting love;*
> *therefore with lovingkindness I have drawn you.*
> *Again I will build you, and you shall be rebuilt."*
> JEREMIAH 31:3–4 NKJV

Quiz 37

Welcome to Babylon. Sorry I—Ezekiel—couldn't have picked a nicer place, but you accept what you're given and try to make the best of it. So, let's see how much you know about me and the book that bears my name. Are you ready? I thought so, because, you see, I'm a prophet! Let's begin.

1. Ezekiel was among the exiles residing by which river?
   a. Styx
   b. Kebar
   c. Gihon
   d. Ahava

2. In Ezekiel's famous vision, he saw creatures with four faces—of a man, a lion, an ox, and a *what*?
   a. horse
   b. Eve
   c. deer
   d. eagle

3. Ezekiel envisioned wheels that had *what* on their rims?

   a. retreads
   b. crystals
   c. eyes
   d. lips

4. In the vision of the wheels, what did the Lord God tell Ezekiel to eat?
   a. a scroll
   b. honey
   c. bread
   d. Dream Whip

5. For the house of Israel, God told Ezekiel to be a *what*?
   a. pane
   b. visionary
   c. watchman
   d. byword

6. In another vision, how did the Spirit of God lift Ezekiel up?
   a. feet first
   b. by his hair
   c. in a whirlwind
   d. with a pay raise

7. God told Ezekiel He would replace the people's hearts of stone with ones of *what*?
   a. an organ donor
   b. life
   c. love
   d. flesh

8. In the valley of dry bones, Ezekiel prophesized to the breath, "Come from" *what*?

   a. "the corners of the earth"
   b. "Listermint"
   c. "the four winds"
   d. "the air, land, and sea"

9. What did the Lord command Ezekiel to write?
   a. on two sticks
   b. on seven scrolls
   c. on one parchment
   d. his autobiography

Quiz 37—Wrap-up

Boy, did I "see" a lot in my lifetime. When you are walking closely with the Lord, you need to keep your eyes open, for you never know when an opportunity to advance the kingdom will arise. Are you paying attention? Daniel did. And he's up next. So I leave you with this reminder:

Make the most of every opportunity. . . .
Don't act thoughtlessly, but understand
what the Lord wants you to do.
Ephesians 5:16–17 NLT

Quiz 38

Salutations! My friends and I wish to welcome you to the quiz featuring me—Daniel! I was a man of prayer, an advisor, and a prophesier. You may be well acquainted with much of my story—but do you know all of it? Let's find out together, shall we? Beginning with question 1.

1. After the Babylonians captured Daniel, he was renamed *what*?
   a. Belteshazzar
   b. Hananiah
   c. Belshazzar
   d. Boone

2. Who was the captain of Nebuchadnezzar's guard?
   a. Ashpenaz
   b. Mishael
   c. Arioch
   d. Bligh

3. Nebuchadnezzar dreamed of a statue that had *what*?

   a. belly and thighs of bronze
   b. chest and arms of gold
   c. head of silver
   d. limitations

4. Before throwing Daniel's friends into the furnace, what did Nebuchadnezzar do?
   a. grabbed a package of marshmallows and a stick
   b. had the furnace heated seven times hotter
   c. ordered the men flogged
   d. commanded the men be disrobed

5. Nebuchadnezzar's second dream was about *what*?
   a. a tree
   b. a horse
   c. sugarplums
   d. a fire in the sky

6. Later, Nebuchadnezzar ate grass like cattle while his hair *what*?
    a. was cowlick-ed
    b. turned gray
    c. grew like an eagle's feathers
    d. fell out in clumps

7. Daniel interpreted handwriting on the wall that read, "MENE" *what*?
    a. "MEENY, MINY, MOE"
    b. "MENE, TEKEL, PARSIN"
    c. "MENE, TASKEL, PARMIN"
    d. "MENE, TAKEL, PERSIN"

8. What king threw Daniel into the lions' den?
    a. Nebuchadnezzar of Babylon
    b. Siegfried of Roy
    c. Darius the Mede
    d. Cyrus the Persian

9. In a weird vision of a ram and a goat, Daniel was standing by the canal named *what*?
    a. Eerie
    b. Ulai
    c. Ahava
    d. Pethor

Quiz 38—Wrap-up

Yes, I was quite the visionary in my day. And although I was under a lot of pressure, I remained faithful to my God, especially in prayer. Are you doing the same?

Three times a day [Daniel] got down on his knees and prayed, giving thanks to his God, just as he had done before.
DANIEL 6:10 NIV

Quiz 39

Ahoy! Jonah, here. Boy, do I have a whale of a quiz for you. Are you prepared to see how much you remember about my book? Great! I hope things go swimmingly for you! Let's launch right into question 1.

1. Jonah was the son of *whom*?
   a. a preacher man
   b. Amittai
   c. Eliakim
   d. Zerubbabel

2. Where was Jonah from?
   a. Bethel
   b. Mizpah
   c. a band of brothers
   d. Gath Hepher

3. Instead of going to Ninevah, Jonah went *where*?

   a. Joppa
   b. Tarshish
   c. fishing
   d. Susa

4. Inside the whale, Jonah called for help "from deep in the" *what*?
   a. "the sea"
   b. "the whale's bowels"
   c. "realm of the dead"
   d. "despair"

5. To walk across Nineveh took *what*?
   a. courage
   b. ten of ya
   c. three days
   d. much money

6. The first thing Jonah proclaimed in Nineveh was, "Forty days" *what*?
    a. "hath September."
    b. "from now Nineveh will be destroyed."
    c. "to repent of your evil!"
    d. "from today, your city will sink into the sea."

7. When God relented from destroying Nineveh, Jonah *what*?
    a. was embarrassed
    b. thought something fishy was going on
    c. left town
    d. became angry

8. What destroyed Jonah's shade?

    a. a worm
    b. a hole in the ozone layer
    c. a woodcutter
    d. a scorching east wind

9. Nineveh had 120,000 people who couldn't *what*?
    a. get fire insurance
    b. read or write
    c. tell their right hand from their left
    d. obey God's commandments

Quiz 39—Wrap-up

Quite a fish story, don't you think? God's love and compassion—for us as a people and as individuals—is really amazing. Have you thanked Him lately? Make it a point to do so today. Meanwhile, I leave you in the capable hands of Elizabeth. And I'll see you later on the other shore!

As far as the east is from the west,
so far has He removed our transgressions from us.
PSALM 103:12 AMP

Quiz 40

Welcome to the New Testament portion of our program! We're going to begin with me, Elizabeth. I was a godly woman who had no idea what God was going to do with and through me. Do you ever feel the same way? Just keep your eyes open and watch for God to work. For now, get your pencil moving and watch where you can make your mark in this next quiz.

1. Elizabeth's story is told in *what*?
    a. *Pride and Prejudice*
    b. Luke 1
    c. Mark 1
    d. Matthew 1

2. Elizabeth was married to Zechariah, who belonged to the priestly division of *whom*?
    a. Pope John Paul I
    b. Hakkoz
    c. Abijah
    d. Maaziah

3. An angel appeared to Zechariah on the right side of *what*?

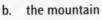

    a. the Law
    b. the mountain
    c. the temple
    d. the altar of incense

4. The angel told Zechariah that John the Baptist would go in the power of *whom*?
    a. Elijah
    b. Aaron
    c. the Lord
    d. an attorney

5. After his confrontation with the angel, Zechariah could no longer *what*?
    a. see
    b. eat wings
    c. hear
    d. speak

6. A now-pregnant Elizabeth hid *what*?
    a. for protection
    b. for five months
    c. Easter eggs
    d. yeast

7. Elizabeth was of the daughters of *whom*?
    a. Caleb
    b. David
    c. Aaron
    d. the American Revolution

8. Mary came to visit Elizabeth and stayed for *what*?

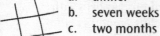

    a. dinner
    b. seven weeks
    c. two months
    d. three months

9. Zechariah prophesied that his son John would be called "the prophet of" *what*?
    a. "the Most High"
    b. "the Dayspring"
    c. "the Messiah"
    d. "Elijah"

Quiz 40—Wrap-up

Even when we are barren, the Lord fills our lives with miracles untold, uncountable. Feeling empty? Pray for the Lord to pile His blessings upon you. Then wait to see what will happen! I was blessed with John. What will you receive?

> *The angel reassured him, "Don't fear. . . .*
> *Your prayer has been heard."*
> LUKE 1:13 MSG

Quiz 41

Greetings from the desert. You've already met my mother,
Elizabeth. Now I, John the Baptist, get to quiz you on my
adventures. Are you ready for anything? Great! Let's get
started.

1. John the Baptist preached in the wilderness of *what*?
    a. Sin
    b. Judea
    c. Shur
    d. Paran

2. What prophet foresaw the coming of a preparer of the way, John?
    a. John Foresight
    b. Amos
    c. Elijah
    d. Isaiah

3. What angel announced John's birth?
    a. Gabriel
    b. Michael
    c. Sarah Fim
    d. Raphael

4. When John saw Pharisees and Sadducees coming to his baptism, he called them *what*?
    a. flotsam of the wrath
    b. brood of vipers
    c. yeast in the bread
    d. snakes in the grass

5. John ate honey and *what*?
    a. wheat germ
    b. flat bread
    c. barley
    d. locusts

6. John baptized Jesus in the *what*?
    a. Jordan River
    b. Sea of Galilee
    c. Profice Sea
    d. Dead Sea

7. Jesus said John came neither eating bread nor drinking wine, yet they say *what*?
    a. "He's anorexic."
    b. "He is Elijah."
    c. "He has a demon."
    d. "He is a Nazirite."

8. To ask John who he was, the Jews of Jerusalem sent priests and *who*?

    a. nuns
    b. Sadducees
    c. Pharisees
    d. Levites

9. At whose request did King Herod have John beheaded?
    a. Herodias
    b. Herodias's daughter
    c. his brother Philip
    d. Pilate

Quiz 41—Wrap-up

Well, I hope you didn't lose your head over that quiz. In
this life there is nothing to be anxious about. Just trust in
God. He'll see you through anything and everything. I've
gotta go, but I'll leave you in good hands with Mary.

> *"Do no fear, for I have redeemed you;*
> *I have summoned you by name; you are mine.*
> *When you pass through the waters,*
> *I will be with you."*
> Isaiah 43:1–2 niv

Quiz 42

Hail there! My name is Mary, and I was the mother of Jesus. Ah, the best Son a mom could ever ask for. My story is bittersweet. Let's see how much general and trivial knowledge you have regarding me and my life. Put your thinking caps on and let's get started.

1. The angel Gabriel came to visit Mary in Nazareth, a town in *where*?
   a. Pennsylvania
   b. Galilee
   c. Samaria
   d. Judea

2. Gabriel told Mary that with God she had found *what*?
   a. religion
   b. delight
   c. mercy
   d. favor

3. When Gabriel came to Mary, Elizabeth had been *what*?

   a. craving pickles
   b. five weeks pregnant
   c. six months pregnant
   d. eight months pregnant

4. As recorded in Matthew, the father of Joseph, Mary's betrothed, was named *what*?
   a. Jacob
   b. Mr. Carpenter
   c. Levi
   d. Jannai

5. The number of generations from the Babylonian exodus to Jesus' birth was *what*?
   a. twelve
   b. thirteen
   c. fourteen
   d. fifteen

6. How many sons did Mary have after Jesus?
    a. none
    b. one
    c. three
    d. four

7. Who greeted Mary, Joseph, and the newborn Jesus at the temple?
    a. Jesus' godparents
    b. Simeon and Anna
    c. the sons of Zebedee
    d. Elizabeth and Zechariah

8. At the wedding Mary attended in Cana, her Son miraculously changed into wine *what*?

    a. Rhine
    b. four barrels of water
    c. five vessels of water
    d. six stone jars of water

9. Witnessing Jesus' crucifixion were His mother Mary, her sister, Mary Magdalene, and another Mary whose husband was named *what*?
    a. Clopas
    b. Chuza
    c. Ananias
    d. Tyler-Mor

Quiz 42—Wrap-up

So, do you see how amazing my story was? I was the most blessed of women. When I heard of Jesus' coming into this world through me, I couldn't help but sing! Why don't you lift your own voice in praise today, thanking the Lord for the good, the bad, and the marvelous!

> *"Oh, how my soul praises the Lord.*
> *How my spirit rejoices in God my Savior!*
> *For he took notice of his lowly servant girl,*
> *and from now on all generations will call me blessed."*
> Luke 1:46–48 NLT

Quiz 43

Grrr. Bow down when you enter my presence, you lowly knave. Herod the Great here, representing all the members of my royal family. We were not friends of the One they called the Christ. Are you familiar with our role in the Gospel stories? Hmm. Not sure, are you? Well, why don't you see what you can do with the next nine questions?

1. Herod the Great ordered the deaths of boys in Bethlehem and its vicinity who *what*?
   a. ate Ramah noodles
   b. were Jewish
   c. were two years old and under
   d. had been visited by shepherds

2. Knowing of Herod's plan, an angel told Joseph to escape with Jesus to *where*?
   a. Witch Mountain
   b. Egypt
   c. Galilee
   d. Judea

3. Herod the Great's son, who ruled Judea in place of his father, was named *what*?

   a. Herod the Not-So-Great
   b. Agrippa
   c. Antipas
   d. Archelaus

4. Herod Antipas, the one who had John the Baptist killed, was married to *whom*?
   a. Antipasta
   b. Herodias
   c. Drusilla
   d. Bernice

5. What was the job title of Herod Antipas?
   a. tetrarch
   b. throne-in-side
   c. senator
   d. patriarch

6. Herod Antipas divorced his first wife to marry the wife of which half brother?

    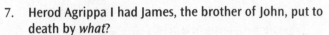

    a. Herod the Halfling
    b. Aretas
    c. Pilate
    d. Philip

7. Herod Agrippa I had James, the brother of John, put to death by *what*?
    a. chocolate
    b. crucifixion
    c. hanging
    d. the sword

8. Because Herod Agrippa did not give praise to God, he *what*?

    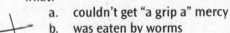

    a. couldn't get "a grip a" mercy
    b. was eaten by worms
    c. "accidentally" drowned
    d. had a heart attack

9. Who is named three times in the Bible as Herod Agrippa II's companion—who tradition says was his sister?

    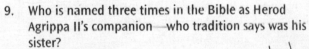

    a. Drusilla
    b. Herodias
    c. Bernice
    d. Cruella de Vil

Quiz 43—Wrap-up

Hmm, in looking back, my family doesn't have a very good history, does it? I guess the moral is to listen to God when He speaks, be it via dreams, angels, wise men, shepherds, disciples, prophets, or He Himself. Well, now I must depart. It was nice, being aboveground for a short while. Now I'll leave you with someone who was definitely more of a saint than I was.

And having been warned by God in a dream not to return to Herod, the magi left for their own country by another way.
MATTHEW 2:12 NASB

Quiz 44

Hello there! Peter here. Before following Jesus, I was a fisherman, minding my own business. Then, all of a sudden, I was in training to be a fisher of *men*! You never know what opportunities are going to come your way. Now I present you with an opportunity to see how much you remember about me from the Bible stories. Ready? Let's see if you can catch some good answers!

1. Jesus first met Peter when he was fishing with his brother named *what*?
   a. Popeye
   b. Andrew
   c. John
   d. Philip

2. The names *Peter* and *Cephas*—both of which Jesus gave to Simon—have meanings related to what thing in nature?
   a. rock
   b. water
   c. clouds
   d. trees

3. Jesus told Peter, "on this rock I will build my church," and it will not be overcome by *what*?
   a. paper or scissors
   b. Satan the father of lies
   c. evilness
   d. the gates of Hades

4. In Jesus' transfiguration, Peter offered to build three shelters for *whom*?
   a. Elijah, Jesus, and Moses
   b. John, Jesus, and Aaron
   c. David, Jesus, and Moses
   d. Peter, Paul, and Mary

5. In Peter's day, what was the temple tax for Jewish males?
   a. one turtledove   c. one talent
   b. two pigeons   d. two drachmas

6. What was Peter's hometown?
    a. St. Petersburg
    b. Capernaum
    c. Nazareth
    d. Bethsaida

7. Peter sliced off the right ear of the high priest's servant named *what*?
    a. Malchus
    b. van Gogh
    c. Caiaphas
    d. Annas

8. After the risen Jesus appeared to the disciples, Peter pulled in a net filled with *what*?
    a. Benings
    b. 123 fish
    c. 153 fish
    d. 173 fish

9. In Acts 3, Peter healed the crippled beggar outside at *what*?
    a. the temple ramp
    b. the upper room
    c. three o'clock in the afternoon
    d. nightfall

Quiz 44—Wrap-up

Well, I hope I didn't talk your ear off. There is a lot more to my story, but you get some idea of what my life was like in this little vignette. Now I've got to run, but I leave you in good hands with Matthew. Before I go, here's a positive thought, just for you! (You can find lots more like it in the Good Book.)

> *By his divine power, God has given us*
> *everything we need for living a godly life.*
> 2 PETER 1:3 NLT

Quiz 45

I'll be with you in a moment.... Okay. Now I'm ready. Sorry, I was just adding up some numbers. Used to be a tax collector, you know. My name is Matthew, author of the first Gospel in the New Testament. Cool, right? Let's see if you can remember some facts about me and my book. Ready?

1. According to the *Amplified Bible*, Jesus first met Matthew when he was sitting in a tax collector's booth *where*?
   a. at H&R Block
   b. in Capernaum
   c. in Bethsaida
   d. in Nazareth

2. In Mark 2:14, Matthew is referred to as "Levi son of" *whom*?
   a. Alphaeus
   b. Strauss
   c. Cephas
   d. Aaron

3. Matthew records Jesus saying, "Blessed are the pure in heart, for they will" *what*?
   a. "be shown mercy"
   b. "inherit the earth"
   c. "be excellent organ donors"
   d. "see God"

4. Who does Matthew list as Jesus' brothers?
   a. the Carpenters
   b. Jesse, Jacob, Judas, and James
   c. James, Joseph, Simon, and Judas
   d. Jeremiah, Joshua, Simon, and Jared

5. Matthew records Jesus telling the disciples to forgive their brothers *what*?
   a. in taxing situations
   b. seventy-seven times
   c. eighty-eight times
   d. ninety-nine times

6. In Matthew 1:21, an angel told Joseph to name Mary's son Jesus because *what*?
   a. there were already too many Josephs in the family
   b. He will save people from their sins
   c. Jesus means "God is with us"
   d. He would become king

7. In Matthew 25, what did two out of three men do with their talents?
   a. became contestants on *America's Got Talents*
   b. tripled their money
   c. doubled their money
   d. invested their money in a bank

8. How many chapters are in the book of Matthew?
   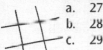
   a. 27
   b. 28
   c. 29
   d. 30

9. In the Bible, the final mention of Matthew's name appears in *where*?
   a. his last will and "testament"
   b. the Gospel of John
   c. the book of Acts
   d. Revelation

Quiz 45—Wrap-up

I hope that wasn't overtaxing for you. I promised Jesus I wouldn't do that anymore. After I met Him, my entire life changed. Has yours? I hope so. Next in line is another Gospel writer—Mark (he's used to coming after me). Meanwhile, here's a little something to help you with priorities:

> *"Seek first God's kingdom and what God wants.*
> *Then all your other needs will be met as well."*
> Matthew 6:33 ncv

Quiz 46

John Mark here. Wondering who I am? Well, I was the author of the Gospel of Mark and doer of so much more! But I don't want to give away all my secrets here. Instead, I'll quiz you! Let's get started.

1. The Gospel of Mark records Jesus healing a blind man by doing *what*?

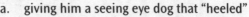

   a. giving him a seeing eye dog that "heeled"
   b. taking splinters out of his eyes
   c. spitting on his eyes
   d. rubbing mud on his eyes

2. After being healed, the blind man in Mark 8 said, "I see" *what*?
   a. "men like trees, walking"
   b. "clearly now"
   c. "that you are the Messiah"
   d. "dead people"

3. The Gospel of Mark records that Jesus drove *what* out of Mary Magdalene?
   a. three demons
   b. seven demons
   c. ten demons
   d. swine flu (pigs really can fly!)

4. Mark lists as bringing spices to Jesus' tomb three women named *what*?
   a. Julia the Child, Martha the Steward, and Rachel of Ray
   b. Mary Magdalene, another Mary, and Salome
   c. Mary, Martha, and Priscilla
   d. Joanna, Mary Magdalene, and another Mary

5. What was the name of John Mark's mom?
   a. Joanna
   b. Tabitha
   c. Dorcas
   d. Mary

6. John Mark had a cousin named Barnabas, whose name means "Son of" *what*?
    a. Agun
    b. Thunder
    c. Encouragement
    d. Wonders

7. John Mark deserted missionaries Paul and Barnabas *where*?
    a. Pamphylia
    b. Cyprus
    c. Salamis
    d. Antioch

8. John Mark was with an imprisoned Paul in Colosse, along with a man named *what*?
    a. Barnabas
    b. John
    c. James
    d. Aristarchus

9. In 2 Timothy, why does an imprisoned Paul request that Mark be sent to him?
    a. "I have forgiven him."
    b. "He is helpful to me."
    c. "He's my 'pen' pal."
    d. "I need my coat."

Quiz 46—Wrap-up

That about wraps it up. I hope you had fun with this quiz. Even if you didn't answer all the questions correctly, perhaps you learned something along the way. Believe me, I made lots of mistakes. Thank God for forgiveness! And say hello to Luke for me. He's next in line—as always!

> *"If you hold anything against anyone,*
> *forgive them, so that your Father in heaven*
> *may forgive you your sins."*
> MARK 11:25 NIV

Quiz 47

Say, "Ahhh." Well, you look right as rain, my friend. Luke here. I'm a doctor, as well as the author of the third Gospel in the New Testament and the book of Acts. Man, the accounts I investigated and then wrote about...some pretty amazing stuff! How much of it can you recall without checking the main fact source—the Bible? Let's find out, shall we?

1. Both the Gospel of Luke and the book of Acts are addressed to Luke's friend named *what*?
   a. Demas
   b. Han Solo
   c. Theophilus
   d. Onesimus

2. Luke writes that when Jesus began his ministry, He was *what*?
   a. a novice
   b. thirty years old
   c. thirty-three years old
   d. thirty-five years old

3. Luke 3 traces Jesus' lineage back to *whom*?

   a. Adam
   b. Noah
   c. David
   d. the Pilgrims

4. In Luke 10, what does Jesus say to Martha?
   a. "Are you an unjust Stewart?"
   b. "Take away the stone."
   c. "Your brother will live again."
   d. "Only one thing is necessary."

5. In Luke 13, Jesus heals a woman who for eighteen years had been *what*?
   a. crippled
   b. bleeding
   c. uninsured
   d. having seizures

6. In Luke 16, Jesus told a parable of a rich man and of a beggar named *what*?

    a. Stephanas
    b. Lazarus
    c. Caiaphas
    d. Cornelius

7. In Luke 8, Jesus healed the synagogue ruler Jairus's *what*?

    a. servant
    b. mother-in-law
    c. daughter
    d. whiplash

8. Luke 8 mentions Joanna's husband (manager of Herod's household), whose name was *what*?

    a. Demas
    b. Silas
    c. Johnny Carson
    d. Chuza

9. In Acts 27, how many passengers eventually shipwrecked off Malta?

    a. 153
    b. 179
    c. 213
    d. 276

Quiz 47—Wrap-up

So, how did you do? Did that quiz get your pulse racing? Do I need to check your blood pressure? I'm sure you did well. Time for me to head out. Remember to keep yourself well in the Word. And if you need help understanding, just send Jesus an SOS. God bless!

*Then [Jesus] opened their minds so
they could understand the Scriptures.*
LUKE 24:45 NIV

Quiz 48

Oh, hello. Sorry. I was so busy counting the money in our treasury that I didn't see you there. My name is Judas. I guess you could say I was the Benedict Arnold of the New Testament, although I wasn't the *only* one who deserted Jesus. Okay, so I made a few really bad choices in my life. I guess you know all about that. Or do you? Let's find out.

1. Judas's betrayal of Jesus fulfilled Psalm 41:9, which says "Even my own familiar friend. . .has lifted" *what*?
    a. "my wallet"
    b. "up his heel against me"
    c. "his eyes to Satan"
    d. "himself above me"

2. What was Judas's dad's first name?
    a. Escargot
    b. Jonah
    c. Simon
    d. James

3. As holder of the money box, Judas complained about the cost of *what*?

    a. discipleship
    b. oil
    c. the Last Supper
    d. Mary's perfume

4. For handing over Jesus, what did the chief priests pay Judas?
    a. traitor bonds
    b. thirty silver coins
    c. forty silver coins
    d. fifty silver coins

5. The exact monetary profit Judas gained for his betrayal was predicted by which prophet?
    a. Isaiah
    b. Nehemiah
    c. Zechariah
    d. Jeremiah

6. Judas promised the priests he'd betray Jesus in the absence of *what*?
    a. the multitude
    b. malice
    c. the other disciples
    d. the scribes

7. The soldiers arresting Jesus took Him to the high priest named *what*?
    a. Annas
    b. Caiaphas
    c. Theophilus
    d. Matthias

8. The field in which Judas hanged himself was called the Field of Blood, which in Aramaic is *what*?

    a. Akeldama
    b. Gabbatha
    c. Gerasa
    d. Plasmalea

9. Which man was chosen to replace Judas as a disciple?
    a. Substitutias
    b. Barsabbas
    c. Justus
    d. Matthias

Quiz 48—Wrap-up

Well, that's the end of my sad, sad tale. Tragic, isn't it?
Yet my life was a product of the choices I'd made. What
choices are you making today? Take my advice: follow
Jesus wholeheartedly. Never give in to the dark side. Now
I leave you in the hands of Paul, who started out on the
wrong road in life but ended up choosing the right Way.
A better man than I!

Wherever your treasure is,
there the desires of your heart will also be.
MATTHEW 6:21 NLT

Quiz 49

Greetings, fellow traveler! Amazing that we'd both meet here on the same road. My name is Paul (aka Saul). And my story is pretty spectacular. It begins in the book of Acts. Are you ready to take a side trip into my life? Great! I'm ready when you are!

1. The man who trained Paul in the Jewish law was named *what*?
   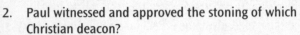
   a. Obi-Wan Kenobi
   b. Gallio
   c. Gamaliel
   d. Crispus

2. Paul witnessed and approved the stoning of which Christian deacon?
   a. Phillips
   b. Stephen
   c. Justus
   d. Barsabbas

3. A light flashed from heaven while Paul was traveling down the road to *where*?

   a. ruin
   b. Jerusalem
   c. Bethany
   d. Damascus

4. Ananias removed the scales from Paul's eyes on the street named *what*?
   a. Straight Street
   b. Shuck Alley
   c. Main Street
   d. Broad Street

5. Paul prayed for a Jewish sorcerer named Elymas to become *what*?
   a. blind
   b. leprous
   c. converted
   d. an outcast

6. In Athens, Paul found an altar with an inscription that read *what*?
    a. Give Me Your Tired, Your Poor
    b. To Our God Zeus
    c. To the Goddess Athena
    d. To an Unknown God

7. Performing exorcisms were the sons of the Jewish priest Sceva, who were *what*?
    a. from Laodicca
    b. seven in number
    c. working hard for demonee
    d. silversmiths

8. Guarded by a soldier, Paul stayed in Rome for *what*?
    a. a fountain of trevi-al reasons
    b. the sake of an imprisoned Silas
    c. two years
    d. a meeting with proconsul Sergius Paulus

9. Which tribe did Paul come from?
    a. Benjamin
    b. Dan
    c. Asher Kutcher
    d. Judah

Quiz 49—Wrap-up

Wow! What a life I led! And we didn't even begin to discuss my many letters, which are now part of the Bible. Well, perhaps some other time. Before you head on to meet up with John, I leave you with this bit of empowerment, which should be part of your daily mantra:

> *I can do all things through*
> *Christ which strengtheneth me.*
> PHILIPPIANS 4:13 KJV

Quiz 50

So you saved me, John, for last! Well, I'm about to give you a great revelation. I'm sure you love my book, a bestseller called the Gospel of John. And I've got a few others. But I don't want to give away too much information here. Instead, let's see how much you know about me and my life work. Ready? Let's go!

1. Who was John's brother?
    a. Adams
    b. Mark
    c. James
    d. Andrew

2. John writes that Jesus saw Nathanael sitting *where*?
    a. at the tax collector's booth
    b. under a fig tree
    c. in a boat
    d. by a sycamore

3. Who were John's parents?
    a. Salome and Zebedee
    b. Eunice and Zebedee
    c. Joseph and Rose
    d. Lois and Zebedee

4. John was rebuked for asking Jesus if He wanted *what*?
    a. four bitten fruit
    b. to wash all of John
    c. John to destroy Samaritans with fire
    d. John to save Jesus' life

5. John writes that the woman at the well had *what*?
    a. water on the brain
    b. four husbands
    c. five husbands
    d. six husbands

6. In John 5, Jesus healed a man sitting by a pool near *what*?
   a. River City
   b. the Sheep Gate
   c. the Water Gate
   d. the Fish Gate

7. John records Pilate sitting on the judgment seat at Gabbatha, which means the Stone *what*?
   a. Pavement
   b. of Jacob
   c. of Witnesses
   d. Henge

8. Where was John eventually exiled, where he wrote the book of Revelation?

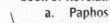

   a. Paphos
   b. Siberia
   c. Malta
   d. Patmos

9. In Revelation 6:8, riding the pale horse was *who*?
   a. the Lone Ranger
   b. Hades
   c. Death
   d. Gabriel

Quiz 50—Wrap-up

Well, that winds up this quiz. . .and this book! Kudos to you if you've gone through all these quizzes. I hope you learned lots along the way. And now we must part. So, for myself and all the other forty-nine quizzers, I bid you adieu and leave you with one final thought and blessing:

> *"God's dwelling place is now among the people,*
> *and he will dwell with them. . . .*
> *He will wipe every tear from their eyes.*
> *There will be no more death or mourning or crying or pain."*
> REVELATION 21:3–4 NIV

Answer Key

Question 1

Quiz 1—c. ("God made two great lights—the greater light to govern the day and the lesser light to govern the night. . .the fourth day." Genesis 1:16–19 NIV)

Quiz 2—d. ("Abraham answered: I did it because I didn't think any of you respected God, and I was sure that someone would kill me to get my wife. Besides, she is my half sister. We have the same father, but different mothers." Genesis 20:11–12 CEV)

Quiz 3—c. ("And Sarai Abram's wife took Hagar her maid the Egyptian. . . and gave her to her husband Abram to be his wife." Genesis 16:3 KJV)

Quiz 4—c. ("This is the genealogy of Terah: Terah begot Abram, Nahor, and Haran. Haran begot Lot." Genesis 11:27 NKJV)

Quiz 5—d. ("Now Abraham was one hundred years old when his son Isaac was born to him. Sarah said, 'God has made laughter for me; everyone who hears will laugh with me.'" Genesis 21:5–6 NASB)

Quiz 6—d. ("The second baby grabbed on to his brother's heel, so they named him Jacob." Genesis 25:26 CEV)

Quiz 7—c. ("But three days later, when their wounds were still sore, two of Jacob's sons, Simeon and Levi, who were Dinah's full brothers, took their swords and entered the town without opposition. Then they slaughtered every male there, 26 including Hamor and his son Shechem." Genesis 34:25–26 NLT)

Quiz 8—b. ("Pharaoh heard about it and tried to kill Moses, but Moses got away to the land of Midian." Exodus 2:15 MSG)

Quiz 9—b. ("Aaron took Elisheba, daughter of Amminadab and sister of Nahshon, as wife." Exodus 6.23 AMP)

Quiz 10—b. ("The next day Moses entered the tent and saw that Aaron's staff, which represented the tribe of Levi, had not only sprouted but had budded, blossomed and produced almonds." Numbers 17:8 NIV)

Quiz 11—c. ("Six of the towns you give them will be Safe Towns where a person who has accidentally killed someone can run for protection. But you will also give the Levites forty-two other towns." Numbers 35:6 CEV)

Quiz 12—d. ("Moses called Hoshea the son of Nun, Joshua." Numbers 13:16 NKJV)

Quiz 13—c. ("And when the children of Israel cried unto the Lord, the Lord raised up a deliverer to the children of Israel, who delivered them, even Othniel the son of Kenaz. . .the Lord raised them up a deliverer, Ehud the son of Gera. . .and after him was Shamgar the son of Anath." Judges 3:9, 15, 31 KJV)

Quiz 14—a. ("Moreover, I have acquired Ruth the Moabitess, the widow of Mahlon, to be my wife. . . ." Ruth 4:10 NASB)

Quiz 15—b. ("This man went from his city year by year to worship and sacrifice to the Lord of hosts at Shiloh, where Hophni and Phinehas, the two sons of Eli, were the Lord's priests." 1 Samuel 1:3 AMP)

Quiz 16—d. ("When Elkanah slept with Hannah, the Lord remembered her plea, and in due time she gave birth to a son. She named him Samuel, for she said, 'I asked the Lord for him.'" 1 Samuel 19–20 NLT)

Quiz 17—c. ("There was a man from the tribe of Benjamin named Kish. He was the son of Abiel, grandson of Zeror, great-grandson of Becorath, great-great-grandson of Aphiah—a Benjaminite of stalwart character. He had a son, Saul, a most handsome young man." 1 Samuel 9:1–2 MSG)

Quiz 18—b. ("The priest replied, 'The sword of Goliath the Philistine, whom you killed in the Valley of Elah, is here. . . .'" 1 Samuel 21:9 NIV)

Quiz 19—a. ("Saul's wife was Ahinoam, the daughter of Ahimaaz. They had three sons: Jonathan, Ishvi, and Malchishua." 1 Samuel 14:49–50 CEV)

Quiz 20—b. ("And Obed begat Jesse, and Jesse begat David." Ruth 4:22 KJV)

Quiz 21—a. ("When your days are fulfilled and you rest with your fathers, I will set up your seed after you, who will come from your body, and I will establish his kingdom. He shall build a house for My name, and I will establish the throne of his kingdom forever." 2 Samuel 7:11–13 NKJV)

Quiz 22—c. ("Absalom the son of Maacah, the daughter of Talmai, king of Geshur. . ." 2 Samuel 3:3 NASB)

Quiz 23—b. ("And David took more concubines and wives out of Jerusalem, after he came from Hebron, and other sons and daughters were born to [him]. And these are the names of those who were born to him in Jerusalem: Shammua, Shobab, Nathan, Solomon. . . ." 2 Samuel 5:13–14 AMP)

Quiz 24—c. ("Solomon ruled in Jerusalem over all Israel for forty years. When he died, he was buried in the City of David, named for his father. Then his son Rehoboam became the next king." 1 Kings 11:42–43 NLT)

Quiz 25—b. ("Asa died and was buried with his ancestors in the City of David. His son Jehoshaphat became king after him." 1 Kings 15:24 MSG)

Quiz 26—d. ("This is what the LORD Almighty, the God of Israel, says about Ahab son of Kolaiah and Zedekiah son of Maaseiah, who are prophesying lies to you in my name: 'I will deliver them into the hands of Nebuchadnezzar king of Babylon, and he will put them to death before your very eyes. Because of them, all the exiles from Judah who are in Babylon will use this curse: "May the LORD treat you like Zedekiah and Ahab, whom the king of Babylon burned in the fire."'" Jeremiah 29:21–22 NIV)

Quiz 27—c. ("Later, the LORD said to Elijah, 'Leave and go across the Jordan River so you can hide near Cherith Creek. You can drink water from the creek, and eat the food I've told the ravens to bring you.'" 1 Kings 17:2–4 CEV)

Quiz 28—a. ("And it shall come to pass, that him that escapeth the sword of Hazael shall Jehu slay." 1 Kings 19:17 KJV)

Quiz 29—b. ("Then he took the mantle of Elijah that had fallen from him, and struck the water, and said, 'Where is the LORD God of Elijah?' And when he also had struck the water, it was divided this way and that; and Elisha crossed over." 2 Kings 2:14 NKJV)

Quiz 30—b. ("When Athaliah the mother of Ahaziah saw that her son was dead, she rose and destroyed all the royal offspring." 2 Kings 11:1 NASB)

Quiz 31—b. ("He removed the high places, broke the images, cut down the Asherim, and broke in pieces the bronze serpent that Moses had made, for until then the Israelites had burned incense to it; but he called it Nehushtan [a bronze trifle]." 2 Kings 18:4 AMP)

Quiz 32—b. ("Many years later, during the reign of King Artaxerxes of Persia, there was a man named Ezra. . . ." Ezra 7:1, 7 NLT; "Early the following spring, in the month of Nisan, during the twentieth year of King Artaxerxes' reign, I was serving the king his wine. . . ." Nehemiah 2:1 NLT)

Quiz 33—d. ("At that time King Xerxes reigned from his royal throne in the citadel of Susa." Esther 1:2 NIV)

Quiz 34—d. ("Many years ago, a man named Job lived in the land of Uz." Job 1:1 CEV)

Quiz 35—b. ("And he sent Eliakim, which was over the household, and Shebna the scribe, and the elders of the priests, covered with sackcloth, to Isaiah the prophet the son of Amoz." 2 Kings 19:2 KJV)

Quiz 36—b. ("Oh, that my head were waters, and my eyes a fountain of tears, that I might weep day and night for the slain of the daughter of my people!" Jeremiah 9:1 NKJV)

Quiz 37—b. ("In my thirtieth year, in the fourth month on the fifth day, while I was among the exiles by the Kebar River, the heavens were opened and I saw visions of God." Ezekiel 1:1 NIV)

Quiz 38—a. ("Then the commander of the officials assigned new names to them; and to Daniel he assigned the name Belteshazzar." Daniel 1:7 NASB)

Quiz 39—b. ("Now the word of the Lord came to Jonah son of Amittai, saying. . ." Jonah 1:1 AMP)

Quiz 40—b. ("When Herod was king of Judea, there was a Jewish priest named Zechariah. He was a member of the priestly order of Abijah, and his wife, Elizabeth, was also from the priestly line of Aaron." Luke 1:5 NLT)

Quiz 41—b. ("While Jesus was living in the Galilean hills, John, called 'the Baptizer,' was preaching in the desert country of Judea." Matthew 3:1 MSG)

Quiz 42—b. ("And in the sixth month the angel Gabriel was sent from God unto a city of Galilee, named Nazareth." Luke 1:26 KJV)

Quiz 43—c. ("Then Herod, when he saw that he was deceived by the wise men, was exceedingly angry; and he sent forth and put to death all the male children who were in Bethlehem and in all its districts, from two years old and under, according to the time which he had determined from the wise men." Matthew 2:16 NKJV)

Quiz 44—b. ("While Jesus was walking along the shore of Lake Galilee, he saw two brothers. One was Simon, also known as Peter, and the other was Andrew." Matthew 4:18 CEV)

Quiz 45—b. ("And Jesus, getting into a boat, crossed to the other side and came to His own town [Capernaum]. . . . As Jesus passed on from there, He saw a man named Matthew sitting at the tax collector's office; and He said to him, Be My disciple [side with My party and follow Me]. And he rose and followed Him." Matthew 9:1, 9 AMP)

Quiz 46—c. ("Jesus took the blind man by the hand and led him out of the village. Then, spitting on the man's eyes, he laid his hands on him and asked, 'Can you see anything now?'" Mark 8:23 CEV)

Quiz 47—c. ("It seemed good to me also, having had perfect understanding of all things from the very first, to write unto thee in order, most excellent Theophilus. . ." Luke 1:3 KJV; "The former treatise have I made, O Theophilus, of all that Jesus began both to do and teach. . ." Acts 1:1 KJV)

Quiz 48—b. ("Even my own familiar friend in whom I trusted, who ate my bread, has lifted up his heel against me." Psalm 41:9 NKJV)

Quiz 49—c. ("I am indeed a Jew, born in Tarsus of Cilicia, but brought up in this city at the feet of Gamaliel, taught according to the strictness of our fathers' law, and was zealous toward God as you all are today." Acts 22:3 NKJV)

Quiz 50—c. ("Going on from there He saw two other brothers, James the son of Zebedee, and John his brother, in the boat with Zebedee their father." Matthew 4:21 NASB)

Question 2

Quiz 1—c. ("But of the tree of the knowledge of good and evil and blessing and calamity you shall not eat, for in the day that you eat of it you shall surely die." Genesis 2:17 AMP)

Quiz 2—b. ("At that time a severe famine struck the land of Canaan, forcing Abram to go down to Egypt, where he lived as a foreigner." Genesis 12:10 NLT)

Quiz 3—a. ("So she called the name of the Lord Who spoke to her, You are a God of seeing, for she said, Have I [not] even here [in the wilderness] looked upon Him Who sees me [and lived]? Or have I here also seen [the future purposes or designs of] Him Who sees me? Therefore the well was called Beer-lahai-roi [A well to the Living One Who sees me]." Genesis 16:13–14 AMP)

Quiz 4—b. ("At the time when Amraphel was king of Shinar, Arioch king of Ellasar, Kedorlaomer king of Elam and Tidal king of Goyim. . ." Genesis 14:1 NIV)

Quiz 5—c. ("So the servant put his hand under the thigh of Abraham his master, and swore to him concerning this matter." Genesis 24:9 NKJV)

Quiz 6—a. ("And Isaac sent away Jacob: and he went to Padanaram unto Laban, son of Bethuel the Syrian, the brother of Rebekah, Jacob's and Esau's mother." Genesis 28:5 KJV)

Quiz 7—a. ("And Judah said to Onan, 'Go in to your brother's wife and marry her, and raise up an heir to your brother.' . . . The thing which he did displeased the LORD; therefore He killed him also. . . . And Tamar went and dwelt in her father's house." Genesis 38:8–11 NKJV)

Quiz 8—c. ("The name of Amram's wife was Jochebed, the daughter of Levi, who was born to Levi in Egypt; and she bore to Amram: Aaron and Moses and their sister Miriam." Numbers 26:59 NASB)

Quiz 9—c. ("And they shall make the ephod of gold, of blue, purple, and scarlet [stuff], and fine twined linen, skillfully woven and worked." Exodus 28:6 AMP)

Quiz 10—c. ("In the first month of the year, the whole community of Israel arrived in the wilderness of Zin and camped at Kadesh. While they were there, Miriam died and was buried." Numbers 20:1 NLT)

Quiz 11—b. ("You shall not covet your neighbor's house. You shall not covet your neighbor's wife, or his male or female servant, his ox or donkey, or anything that belongs to your neighbor." Exodus 20:17 NIV)

Quiz 12—b. ("Our brothers took all the wind out of our sails, telling us, 'The people are bigger and stronger than we are; their cities are huge, their defenses massive—we even saw Anakite giants there!'" Deuteronomy 1:28 MSG)

Quiz 13—b. ("Now she sent and summoned Barak the son of Abinoam from Kedesh-naphtali, and said to him, 'Behold, the LORD, the God of Israel, has commanded, "Go and march to Mount Tabor, and take with you ten thousand men from the sons of Naphtali and from the sons of Zebulun."'" Judges 4:6 NASB)

Quiz 14—b. ("And she said to them, Call me not Naomi [pleasant]; call me Mara [bitter], for the Almighty has dealt very bitterly with me." Ruth 1:20 AMP)

Quiz 15—d. ("Once after a sacrificial meal at Shiloh, Hannah got up and went to pray. Eli the priest was sitting at his customary place beside the entrance of the Tabernacle." 1 Samuel 1:9 NLT)

Quiz 16—d. ("Once the Philistines had seized the Chest of God, they took it from Ebenezer to Ashdod, brought it into the shrine of Dagon, and placed it alongside the idol of Dagon." 1 Samuel 5:1–2 MSG)

Quiz 17—c. ("When all those who had formerly known him saw him prophesying with the prophets, they asked each other, 'What is this that has happened to the son of Kish? Is Saul also among the prophets?'" 1 Samuel 10:11 NIV)

Quiz 18—c. ("The Philistine army had a hero named Goliath who was from the town of Gath and was over nine feet tall." 1 Samuel 17:4 CEV)

Quiz 19—b. ("But Jonathan heard not when his father charged the people with the oath: wherefore he put forth the end of the rod that was in his hand, and dipped it in an honeycomb, and put his hand to his mouth; and his eyes were enlightened." 1 Samuel 14:27 KJV)

Quiz 20—a. ("But Saul had given his daughter Michal, David's wife, to Paltiel son of Laish, who was from Gallim." 1 Samuel 25:44 NIV)

Quiz 21—c. ("But the poor man had nothing, except one little ewe lamb which he had bought and nourished; and it grew up together with him and with his children. It ate of his own food and drank from his own cup and lay in his bosom; and it was like a daughter to him." 2 Samuel 12:3 NKJV)

Quiz 22—a. ("Then Absalom her brother said to her, 'Has Amnon your brother been with you? But now keep silent, my sister, he is your brother; do not take this matter to heart.' So Tamar remained and was desolate in her brother Absalom's house." 2 Samuel 13:20 NASB)

Quiz 23—c. ("And Adonijah feared because of Solomon, and arose and went [to the tabernacle tent on Mt. Zion] and caught hold of the horns of the altar [as a fugitive's refuge]." 1 Kings 1:50 AMP)

Quiz 24—a. ("Rehoboam went to Shechem, where all Israel had gathered to make him king." 1 Kings 12:1 NLT)

Quiz 25—d. ("Jehoshaphat son of Asa became king of Judah in the fourth year of Ahab king of Israel." 1 Kings 22:41 MSG)

Quiz 26—a. ("He not only considered it trivial to commit the sins of Jeroboam son of Nebat, but he also married Jezebel daughter of Ethbaal king of the Sidonians, and began to serve Baal and worship him." 1 Kings 16:31 NIV)

Quiz 27—b. ("'Bring me your son,' Elijah said. Then he took the boy from her arms and carried him upstairs to the room where he was staying. Elijah laid the boy on his bed and prayed, 'Lord God, why did you do such a terrible thing to this woman? She's letting me stay here, and now you've let her son die.' Elijah stretched himself out over the boy three times, while praying, 'Lord God, bring this boy back to life!' The Lord answered Elijah's prayer, and the boy started breathing again." 1 Kings 17:19–22 CEV)

Quiz 28—c. ("And Jehu drew a bow with his full strength, and smote Jehoram between his arms, and the arrow went out at his heart, and he sunk down in his chariot. Then said Jehu to Bidkar his captain, Take up, and cast him in the portion of the field of Naboth the Jezreelite." 2 Kings 9:24–25 KJV)

Quiz 29—c. ("Then he went up from there to Bethel; and as he was going up the road, some youths came from the city and mocked him, and said to him, 'Go up, you baldhead! Go up, you baldhead!' So he turned around and looked at them, and pronounced a curse on them in the name of the LORD. And two female bears came out of the woods and mauled forty-two of the youths." 2 Kings 2:23–24 NASB)

Quiz 30—c. ("But Jehosheba, the daughter of King Jehoram, [half] sister of Ahaziah, stole Joash son of Ahaziah from among the king's sons, who were to be slain, even him and his nurse, and hid them from Athaliah in an inner storeroom for beds; so he was not slain." 2 Kings 11:2 AMP)

Quiz 31—c. ("And it came to pass, when king Hezekiah heard it, that he rent his clothes, and covered himself with sackcloth, and went into the house of the LORD." 2 Kings 19:1 KJV)

Quiz 32—d. ("And there by the Ahava Canal, I gave orders for all of us to fast and humble ourselves before our God. We prayed that he would give us a safe journey and protect us, our children, and our goods as we traveled." Ezra 8:21 NLT)

Quiz 33—b. ("The guests could drink as much as they liked—king's orders!—with waiters at their elbows to refill the drinks. Meanwhile, Queen Vashti was throwing a separate party for women inside King Xerxes' royal palace." Esther 1:8–9 MSG)

Quiz 34—b. ("He had seven sons and three daughters. . . ." Job 1:2 NIV)

Quiz 35—a. ("In the year that King Uzziah died, I had a vision of the LORD. . . ." Isaiah 6:1 KJV)

Quiz 36—c. ("The words of Jeremiah the son of Hilkiah. . .to whom the word of the LORD came in the days of Josiah the son of Amon, king of Judah, in the thirteenth year of his reign." Jeremiah 1:2 NKJV)

Quiz 37—d. ("As for the form of their faces, each had the face of a man; all four had the face of a lion on the right and the face of a bull on the left, and all four had the face of an eagle." Ezekiel 1:10 NASB)

Quiz 38—c. ("Then Daniel returned an answer which was full of prudence and wisdom to Arioch the captain or executioner of the king's guard, who had gone forth to slay the wise men of Babylon." Daniel 2:14 AMP)

Quiz 39—d. ("Jeroboam II recovered the territories of Israel between Lebo-hamath and the Dead Sea, just as the LORD, the God of Israel, had promised through Jonah son of Amittai, the prophet from Gath-hepher." 2 Kings 14:25 NLT)

Quiz 40—c. ("During the rule of Herod, King of Judea, there was a priest assigned service in the regiment of Abijah. His name was Zachariah." Luke 1:5 MSG)

Quiz 41—d. ("This is he who was spoken of through the prophet Isaiah: 'A voice of one calling in the wilderness, "Prepare the way for the Lord, make straight paths for him."'" Matthew 3:3 NIV)

Quiz 42—d. ("And the angel said unto her, Fear not, Mary: for thou hast found favour with God." Luke 1:30 KJV)

Quiz 43—b. ("After the wise men had gone, an angel from the Lord appeared to Joseph in a dream and said, 'Get up! Hurry and take the child and his mother to Egypt! Stay there until I tell you to return, because Herod is looking for the child and wants to kill him.'" Matthew 2:13 CEV)

Quiz 44—a. ("Then Jesus answered him, Blessed (happy, fortunate, and to be envied) are you, Simon Bar-Jonah. For flesh and blood [men] have not revealed this to you, but My Father Who is in heaven. And I tell you, you are Peter [Greek, Petros—a large piece of rock], and on this rock [Greek, petra—a huge rock like Gibraltar] I will build My church." Matthew 16:17–18 AMP; "Andrew then led (brought) Simon to Jesus. Jesus looked at him and said, You are Simon son of John. You shall be called Cephas—which translated is Peter [Stone]." John 1:42 AMP)

Quiz 45—a. ("And as he passed by, he saw Levi the son of Alphaeus sitting at the receipt of custom, and said unto him, Follow me. And he arose and followed him." Mark 2:14 KJV)

Quiz 46—a. ("And he looked up and said, 'I see men like trees, walking.'" Mark 8:24 NKJV)

Quiz 47—b. ("When He began His ministry, Jesus Himself was about thirty years of age." Luke 3:23 NASB)

Quiz 48—c. ("He was speaking of Judas, son of Simon Iscariot, one of the Twelve, who would later betray him." John 6:71 NLT)

Quiz 49—b. ("Yelling and hissing, the mob drowned him out. Now in full stampede, they dragged him out of town and pelted him with rocks. The ringleaders took off their coats and asked a young man named Saul to watch them. As the rocks rained down, Stephen prayed, 'Master Jesus, take my life.' Then he knelt down, praying loud enough for everyone to hear, 'Master, don't blame them for this sin'—his last words. Then he died." Acts 7:57–60 MSG)

Quiz 50—b. ("'How do you know me?' Nathanael asked. Jesus answered, 'I saw you while you were still under the fig tree before Philip called you.'" John 1:48 NIV)

Question 3

Quiz 1—a. ("Seth had a son and named him Enosh." Genesis 4:26 CEV)

Quiz 2—d. ("Abram dwelled in the land of Canaan, and Lot dwelled in the cities of the plain, and pitched his tent toward Sodom." Genesis 13:12 KJV)

Quiz 3—b. ("Therefore Sarah laughed within herself, saying, 'After I have grown old, shall I have pleasure, my lord being old also?'" Genesis 18:12 NKJV)

Quiz 4—c. ("Now the two angels came to Sodom in the evening as Lot was sitting in the gate of Sodom." Genesis 19:1 NASB)

Quiz 5—a. ("Now Rebekah had a brother whose name was Laban." Genesis 24:29 AMP)

Quiz 6—c. ("He named that place Bethel (which means 'house of God'), although the name of the nearby village was Luz." Genesis 28:19 NLT)

Quiz 7—c. ("Reuben heard the brothers talking and intervened to save him, 'We're not going to kill him. No murder. Go ahead and throw him in this cistern out here in the wild, but don't hurt him.'" Genesis 37:21 MSG)

Quiz 8—a. ("Now Moses said to Hobab son of Reuel the Midianite, Moses' father-in-law. . ." Numbers 10:29 NIV)

Quiz 9—a. ("Nadab and Abihu were two of Aaron's sons, but they disobeyed the LORD by burning incense to him on a fire pan, when they were not supposed to. Suddenly the LORD sent fiery flames and burned them to death." Leviticus 10:1–2 CEV)

Quiz 10—a. ("Thus Edom refused to give Israel passage through his border: wherefore Israel turned away from him." Numbers 20:21 KJV)

Quiz 11—a. ("These you may eat: the locust after its kind, the destroying locust after its kind, the cricket after its kind, and the grasshopper after its kind." Leviticus 11:22 NKJV)

Quiz 12—c. ("Be strong and courageous. . . . Only be strong and very courageous. . . . Be strong and courageous! . . . only be strong and courageous." Joshua 1:6, 7, 9, 18 NASB)

Quiz 13—d. ("And behold, as Barak pursued Sisera, Jael came out to meet him and said to him, Come, and I will show you the man you seek. And when he came into her tent, behold, Sisera lay dead, and the tent pin was in his temples." Judges 4:22 AMP)

Quiz 14—d. ("At mealtime Boaz said to her, 'Come over here. Have some bread and dip it in the wine vinegar.'" Ruth 2:14 NIV)

Quiz 15—c. ("As she was praying to the LORD, Eli watched her. Seeing her lips moving but hearing no sound, he thought she had been drinking." 1 Samuel 1:12–13 NLT)

Quiz 16—c. ("'Five gold tumors and five gold rats,' they said, 'to match the number of Philistine leaders. Since all of you—leaders and people—suffered the same plague, make replicas of the tumors and rats that are devastating the country and present them as an offering to the glory of the God of Israel.'" 1 Samuel 6:4 MSG)

Quiz 17—d. ("Kish had a son named Saul, as handsome a young man as could be found anywhere in Israel, and he was a head taller than anyone else." 1 Samuel 9:2 NIV)

Quiz 18—d. ("The Philistine army had a hero named Goliath who was from the town of Gath and was over nine feet tall." 1 Samuel 17:4 CEV)

Quiz 19—d. ("And Jonathan took off the robe that was on him and gave it to David, with his armor, even to his sword and his bow and his belt." 1 Samuel 18:4 NKJV)

Quiz 20—c. ("And David sent and enquired after the woman. And one said, Is not this Bathsheba, the daughter of Eliam, the wife of Uriah the Hittite?" 2 Samuel 11:3 KJV)

Quiz 21—d. ("Then David said to Nathan, 'I have sinned against the LORD.'" 2 Samuel 12:13 NIV)

Quiz 22—b. ("So Absalom had fled and gone to Geshur, and was there three years." 2 Samuel 13:38 NASB)

Quiz 23—b. ("I have also given you what you have not asked, both riches and honor, so that there shall not be any among the kings equal to you all your days." 1 Kings 3:13 AMP)

Quiz 24—c. ("Meanwhile, Rehoboam son of Solomon was king in Judah. He was forty-one years old when he became king." 1 Kings 14:21 NLT)

Quiz 25—c. ("Shaken, Jehoshaphat prayed. He went to GOD for help and ordered a nationwide fast." 2 Chronicles 20:3 MSG)

Quiz 26—d. ("Ahab went to meet Elijah. When he saw Elijah, he said to him, 'Is that you, you troubler of Israel?'" 1 Kings 18:16–17 NIV)

Quiz 27—d. ("As Obadiah was walking along, he met Elijah. Obadiah recognized him, bowed down, and asked, 'Elijah, is it really you?' 'Yes. Go tell Ahab I'm here.' Obadiah replied: 'King Ahab would kill me if I told him that.'" 1 Kings 18:7–9 CEV)

Quiz 28—d. ("And Jehu drew a bow with his full strength, and smote Jehoram between his arms, and the arrow went out at his heart, and he sunk down in his chariot." 2 Kings 9:24 KJV)

Quiz 29—a. ("A certain woman of the wives of the sons of the prophets cried out to Elisha. . . . Then she came and told the man of God. And he said, 'Go, sell the oil and pay your debt; and you and your sons live on the rest.'" 2 Kings 4:1–7 NKJV)

Quiz 30—d. ("She looked and behold, the king was standing by the pillar, according to the custom, with the captains and the trumpeters beside the king; and all the people of the land rejoiced and blew trumpets. Then Athaliah tore her clothes and cried, 'Treason! Treason!'" 2 Kings 11:14 NASB)

Quiz 31—d. ("And it all came to pass, for that night the Angel of the Lord went forth and slew 185,000 in the camp of the Assyrians; and when [the living] arose early in the morning, behold, all these were dead bodies. So Sennacherib king of Assyria departed and returned and dwelt at Nineveh." 2 Kings 19:35–36 AMP)

Quiz 32—a. ("When I heard this, I tore my tunic and cloak, pulled hair from my head and beard and sat down appalled." Ezra 9:3 NIV)

Quiz 33—d. ("Esther was the daughter of Abihail." Esther 2:15 NLT)

Quiz 34—a. ("Sometime later, while Job's children were having one of their parties at the home of the oldest son, a messenger came to Job and said, 'The oxen were plowing and the donkeys grazing in the field next to us when Sabeans attacked. They stole the animals and killed the field hands.'" Job 1:14–15 MSG)

Quiz 35—d. ("In the year that King Uzziah died, I saw the Lord, high and exalted, seated on a throne; and the train of his robe filled the temple." Isaiah 6:1 NIV)

Quiz 36—b. ("The heart is deceitful above all things, and desperately wicked: who can know it?" Jeremiah 17:9 KJV)

Quiz 37—c. ("The rims of the wheels were large and had eyes all the way around them." Ezekiel 1:18 CEV)

Quiz 38—a. ("This image's head was of fine gold, its chest and arms of silver, its belly and thighs of bronze." Daniel 2:32 NKJV)

Quiz 39—b. ("But Jonah rose up to flee to Tarshish from the presence of the LORD." Jonah 1:3 NASB)

Quiz 40—d. ("And there appeared to him an angel of the Lord, standing at the right side of the altar of incense." Luke 1:11 AMP)

Quiz 41—a. ("Then the angel said, 'I am Gabriel! I stand in the very presence of God. It was he who sent me to bring you this good news!'" Luke 1:19 NLT)

Quiz 42—c. ("And did you know that your cousin Elizabeth conceived a son, old as she is? Everyone called her barren, and here she is six months pregnant!" Luke 1:36 MSG)

Quiz 43—d. ("But when he heard that Archelaus did reign in Judaea in the room of his father Herod, he was afraid to go thither: notwithstanding, being warned of God in a dream, he turned aside into the parts of Galilee." Matthew 2:22 KJV)

Quiz 44—d. ("And I tell you that you are Peter, and on this rock I will build my church, and the gates of Hades will not overcome it." Matthew 16:18 NIV)

Quiz 45—d. ("God blesses those people whose hearts are pure. They will see him!" Matthew 5:8 CEV)

Quiz 46—b. ("Now when Jesus was risen early the first day of the week, he appeared first to Mary Magdalene, out of whom he had cast seven devils." Mark 16:9 KJV)

Quiz 47—a. ("Now Jesus Himself began His ministry at about thirty years of age, being (as was supposed) the son of Joseph, the son of Heli. . .the son of Enosh, the son of Seth, the son of Adam, the son of God." Luke 3:23–38 NKJV)

Quiz 48—d. ("Mary then took a pound of very costly perfume of pure nard, and anointed the feet of Jesus and wiped His feet with her hair; and the house was filled with the fragrance of the perfume.

But Judas Iscariot, one of His disciples, who was intending to betray Him, said, 'Why was this perfume not sold for three hundred denarii and given to poor people?'" John 12:3–5 NASB)

Quiz 49—d. ("Now as he traveled on, he came near to Damascus, and suddenly a light from heaven flashed around him." Acts 9:3 AMP)

Quiz 50—a. ("A short distance down the beach they came upon another pair of brothers, James and John, Zebedee's sons." Matthew 4:21 MSG; "Among them were Mary Magdalene, Mary the mother of James and Joseph, and the mother of the Zebedee brothers." Matthew 27:56 MSG; "There were women watching from a distance, among them Mary Magdalene, Mary the mother of the younger James and Joses, and Salome." Mark 15:40 MSG)

Question 4

Quiz 1—b. ("Nevertheless, death reigned from the time of Adam to the time of Moses, even over those who did not sin by breaking a command, as did Adam, who is a pattern of the one to come." Romans 5:14 NIV)

Quiz 2—c. ("King Melchizedek of Salem was a priest of God Most High." Genesis 14:18 CEV)

Quiz 3—d. ("And Abraham was ninety years old and nine, when he was circumcised in the flesh of his foreskin. And Ishmael his son was thirteen years old, when he was circumcised in the flesh of his foreskin. . . . And Abraham circumcised his son Isaac being eight days old, as God had commanded him." Genesis 17:24–25; 21:4 KJV)

Quiz 4—d. ("And they struck the men who were at the doorway of the house with blindness, both small and great, so that they became weary trying to find the door." Genesis 19:11 NKJV)

Quiz 5—c. ("Isaac was forty years old when he took Rebekah, the daughter of Bethuel the Aramean of Paddan-aram, the sister of Laban the Aramean, to be his wife." Genesis 25:20 NASB)

Quiz 6—d. ("When Leah saw that she had ceased to bear, she gave Zilpah her maid to Jacob as a [secondary] wife." Genesis 30:9 AMP)

Quiz 7—a. ("He then restored the chief cup-bearer to his former position, so he could again hand Pharaoh his cup." Genesis 40:21 NLT)

Quiz 8—b. ("So GOD said, 'What's that in your hand?' 'A staff.' 'Throw it on the ground.' He threw it. It became a snake. . . . GOD then said, 'Put your hand inside your shirt.' He slipped his hand under his shirt, then took it out. His hand had turned leprous, like snow. He said, 'Put your hand back under your shirt.' He did it, then took it back out—as healthy as before. 'So if they don't trust you and aren't convinced by the first sign, the second sign should do it. But if it doesn't, if even after these two signs they don't trust you and listen to your message, take some water out of the Nile and pour it out on the dry land; the Nile water that you pour out will turn to blood when it hits the ground.'" Exodus 4:2–3, 6–9 MSG)

Quiz 9—a. ("Make two trumpets of hammered silver, and use them for calling the community together and for having the camps set out." Numbers 10:2 NIV)

Quiz 10—d. ("And Aaron the priest went up into mount Hor at the commandment of the LORD, and died there." Numbers 33:38 KJV)

Quiz 11—b. ("Before you are convicted of a crime, at least two witnesses must be able to testify that you did it." Deuteronomy 19:15 CEV)

Quiz 12—b. ("But she had brought them up to the roof of the house, and hid them with the stalks of flax, which she had laid in order upon the roof." Joshua 2:6 KJV)

Quiz 13—c. ("Look, I shall put a fleece of wool on the threshing floor; if there is dew on the fleece only, and it is dry on all the ground, then I shall know that You will save Israel by my hand, as You have said." Judges 6:37 NKJV)

Quiz 14—c. ("'The LORD bless him!' Naomi said to her daughter-in-law. 'He has not stopped showing his kindness to the living and the dead.' She added, 'That man is our close relative; he is one of our guardian-redeemers.'" Ruth 2:20 NIV)

Quiz 15—a. ("So the sin of these young men was very serious in the LORD's sight, for they treated the LORD's offerings with contempt." 1 Samuel 2:17 NLT)

Quiz 16—c. ("Samuel gave solid leadership to Israel his entire life. Every year he went on a circuit from Bethel to Gilgal to Mizpah. He gave leadership to Israel in each of these places. But always he would return to Ramah, where he lived, and preside from there." 1 Samuel 7:15–17 MSG)

Quiz 17—a. ("The name of the commander of Saul's army was Abner son of Ner, and Ner was Saul's uncle." 1 Samuel 14:50 NIV)

Quiz 18—d. ("Goliath came out and gave his challenge every morning and every evening for forty days." 1 Samuel 17:16 CEV)

Quiz 19—b. ("Then Jonathan said to David, To morrow is the new moon: and thou shalt be missed, because thy seat will be empty. And when thou hast stayed three days, then thou shalt go down quickly, and come to the place where thou didst hide thyself when the business was in hand, and shalt remain by the stone Ezel. And

I will shoot three arrows on the side thereof, as though I shot at a mark." 1 Samuel 20:18–20 KJV)

Quiz 20—d. ("Then Achish said to his servants, 'Look, you see the man is insane. Why have you brought him to me?'" 1 Samuel 21:14 NKJV)

Quiz 21—b. ("Then it happened on the seventh day that the child died. And the servants of David were afraid to tell him that the child was dead, for they said, 'Behold, while the child was still alive, we spoke to him and he did not listen to our voice. How then can we tell him that the child is dead, since he might do himself harm!'" 2 Samuel 12:18 NASB)

Quiz 22—b. ("And when he cut the hair of his head, he weighed it— for at each year's end he cut it, because its weight was a burden to him—and it weighed 200 shekels by the king's weight." 2 Samuel 14:26 AMP)

Quiz 23—d. ("Hiram had previously provided all the cedar and cypress timber and gold that Solomon had requested." 1 Kings 9:11 NLT)

Quiz 24—b. ("And king Solomon raised a levy out of all Israel; and the levy was thirty thousand men. And he sent them to Lebanon, ten thousand a month by courses: a month they were in Lebanon, and two months at home." 1 Kings 5:13–14 KJV; "Thy father made our yoke grievous: now therefore make thou the grievous service of thy father, and his heavy yoke which he put upon us, lighter, and we will serve thee. . . . And now whereas my father did lade you with a heavy yoke, I will add to your yoke: my father hath chastised you with whips, but I will chastise you with scorpions." 1 Kings 12:4–11 KJV)

Quiz 25—b. ("Do not be afraid or discouraged because of this vast army. For the battle is not yours, but God's." 2 Chronicles 20:15 NIV)

Quiz 26—c. ("Ahab replied, 'If you do these things, I'll let you go free.' Then they signed a peace treaty, and Ahab let Benhadad go." 1 Kings 20:34 CEV)

Quiz 27—a. ("And Elijah said unto them, Take the prophets of Baal; let not one of them escape. And they took them: and Elijah brought them down to the brook Kishon, and slew them there." 1 Kings 18:40 KJV)

Quiz 28—b. ("Then Jehu said to Bidkar his captain. . ." 2 Kings 9:25 NKJV)

Quiz 29—c. ("Now Naaman, captain of the army of the king of Aram, was a great man with his master, and highly respected, because by him the LORD had given victory to Aram. The man was also a valiant warrior, but he was a leper. . . . Elisha sent a messenger to him, saying, 'Go and wash in the Jordan seven times, and your flesh will be restored to you and you will be clean. . . .' So he went down and dipped himself seven times in the Jordan, according to the word of the man of God; and his flesh was restored like the flesh of a little child and he was clean." 2 Kings 5:1–14 NASB)

Quiz 30—b. ("Joash was seven years old when he began to reign." 2 Kings 11:21 AMP)

Quiz 31—a. ("One day while he was worshiping in the temple of his god Nisroch, his sons Adrammelech and Sharezer killed him with their swords." 2 Kings 19:37 NLT)

Quiz 32—d. ("All the men of Judah and Benjamin met in Jerusalem within the three days. It was the twentieth day of the ninth month. They all sat down in the plaza in front of The Temple of God. Because of the business before them, and aggravated by the buckets of rain coming down on them, they were restless, uneasy, and anxious." Ezra 10:9 MSG)

Quiz 33—c. ("When Haman saw that Mordecai would not kneel down or pay him honor, he was enraged." Esther 3:5 NIV)

Quiz 34—d. ("That servant was still speaking, when a fourth one dashed up and said, 'Your children were having a feast and drinking wine at the home of your oldest son, when suddenly a windstorm from the desert blew the house down, crushing all of your children.'" Job 1:18–19 CEV)

Quiz 35—c. ("Then flew one of the seraphims unto me, having a live coal in his hand, which he had taken with the tongs from off the altar: And he laid it upon my mouth." Isaiah 6:6 KJV)

Quiz 36—d. ("The word which came to Jeremiah from the LORD, saying: 'Arise and go down to the potter's house, and there I will cause you to hear My words.'" Jeremiah 18:1–2 NKJV)

Quiz 37—a. ("Then He said to me, 'Son of man, eat what you find; eat this scroll, and go, speak to the house of Israel.'" Ezekiel 3:1 NASB)

Quiz 38—b. ("Then Nebuchadnezzar was full of fury and his facial expression was changed [to antagonism] against Shadrach, Meshach, and Abednego. Therefore he commanded that the furnace should be heated seven times hotter than it was usually heated." Daniel 3:19 AMP)

Quiz 39—c. ("In my distress I called to the LORD, and he answered me. From deep in the realm of the dead I called for help, and you listened to my cry." Jonah 2:2 NIV)

Quiz 40—a. ("He will be a man with the spirit and power of Elijah." Luke 1:17 NLT)

Quiz 41—b. ("But when he saw many of the Pharisees and Sadducees coming to his baptism, he said to them, 'Brood of vipers! Who warned you to flee from the wrath to come?'" Matthew 3:7 NKJV)

Quiz 42—a. ("Jacob had Joseph, Mary's husband, the Mary who gave birth to Jesus, the Jesus who was called Christ." Matthew 1:16 MSG)

Quiz 43—b. ("Now Herod had arrested John and bound him and put him in prison because of Herodias, his brother Philip's wife, for John had been saying to him: 'It is not lawful for you to have her.'" Matthew 14:3–4 NIV)

Quiz 44—a. ("So Peter said to him, 'Lord, it is good for us to be here! Let us make three shelters, one for you, one for Moses, and one for Elijah.'" Matthew 17:4 CEV)

Quiz 45—c. ("Isn't this the carpenter's son? Isn't his mother's name Mary, and aren't his brothers James, Joseph, Simon and Judas?" Matthew 13:55 NIV)

Quiz 46—b. ("And when the sabbath was past, Mary Magdalene, and Mary the mother of James, and Salome, had bought sweet spices, that they might come and anoint him." Mark 16:1 KJV)

Quiz 47—d. ("But only one thing is necessary. Mary has chosen what is best, and it will not be taken away from her." Luke 10:42 CEV)

Quiz 48—b. ("Then when Judas, who had betrayed Him, saw that He had been condemned, he felt remorse and returned the thirty pieces of silver to the chief priests and elders." Matthew 27:3 NASB)

Quiz 49—a. ("And the Lord said to him, Get up and go to the street called Straight and ask at the house of Judas for a man of Tarsus named Saul, for behold, he is praying [there]." Acts 9:11 AMP)

Quiz 50—c. ("When James and John saw this, they said to Jesus, 'Lord, should we call down fire from heaven to burn them up?' But Jesus turned and rebuked them." Luke 9:54–55 NLT)

Question 5

Quiz 1—d. ("The Nephilim were on the earth in those days—and also afterward—when the sons of God went to the daughters of humans and had children by them. They were the heroes of old, men of renown." Genesis 6:4 NIV)

Quiz 2—a. ("And the scripture was fulfilled that says, 'Abraham believed God, and it was credited to him as righteousness,' and he was called God's friend." James 2:23 NIV)

Quiz 3—c. ("The LORD said, 'Go get Isaac, your only son, the one you dearly love! Take him to the land of Moriah, and I will show you a mountain where you must sacrifice him to me on the fires of an altar.'" Genesis 22:2 CEV)

Quiz 4—b. ("But his wife looked back from behind him, and she became a pillar of salt." Genesis 19:26 KJV)

Quiz 5—d. ("Two nations are in your womb; and two peoples will be separated from your body." Genesis 25:23 NASB)

Quiz 6—c. ("The sons of Leah: Reuben, Jacob's firstborn, Simeon, Levi, Judah, Issachar, and Zebulun." Genesis 35:23 AMP)

Quiz 7—b. ("When the Babylonian army left Jerusalem because of Pharaoh's approaching army, Jeremiah started to leave the city on his way to the territory of Benjamin. . . . They were furious with Jeremiah and had him flogged and imprisoned in the house of Jonathan the secretary." Jeremiah 37:11–15 NLT)

Quiz 8—d. ("Just as Jannes and Jambres opposed Moses, so these men also oppose the truth, men of depraved mind, rejected in regard to the faith." 2 Timothy 3:8 NASB)

Quiz 9—d. ("The Israelites named it manna (What is it?). It looked like coriander seed, whitish. And it tasted like a cracker with honey." Exodus 16:31 MSG)

Quiz 10—b. ("Aaron shall be gathered unto his people: for he shall not enter into the land which I have given unto the children of Israel, because ye rebelled against my word at the water of Meribah." Numbers 20:24 KJV)

Quiz 11—d. (". . .from the tribe of Judah, Caleb the son of Jephunneh." Numbers 13:6 NKJV)

Quiz 12—d. ("The waters which were flowing down from above stood and rose up in one heap, a great distance away at Adam, the city that is beside Zarethan." Joshua 3:16 NASB)

Quiz 13—a. ("So Gideon took the men down to the water. There the LORD told him, 'Separate those who lap the water with their tongues as a dog laps from those who kneel down to drink.' Three hundred of them drank from cupped hands, lapping like dogs. All the rest got down on their knees to drink. The LORD said to Gideon, 'With the three hundred men that lapped I will save you and give the Midianites into your hands.'" Judges 7:5–7 NIV)

Quiz 14—b. ("Ruth gleaned in the field until evening. When she threshed out what she had gathered, she ended up with nearly a full sack of barley!" Ruth 2:17 MSG)

Quiz 15—c. ("Wherefore the LORD God of Israel saith. . .there shall not be an old man in thine house. . .and the man of thine, whom I shall not cut off from mine altar, shall be to consume thine eyes, and to grieve thine heart. . . . And this shall be a sign unto thee, that shall come upon thy two sons, on Hophni and Phinehas; in one day they shall die both of them." 1 Samuel 2:30–36 KJV)

Quiz 16—a. ("Samuel had two sons. The older one was Joel, and the younger one was Abijah. When Samuel was getting old, he let them be leaders at Beersheba. But they were not like their father. They were dishonest and accepted bribes to give unfair decisions." 1 Samuel 8:1–3 CEV)

Quiz 17—b. ("I greatly regret that I have set up Saul as king, for he has turned back from following Me, and has not performed My commandments." 1 Samuel 15:11 NKJV)

Quiz 18—b. ("He said to David, 'Am I a dog, that you come at me with sticks?' And the Philistine cursed David by his gods." 1 Samuel 17:43 NIV)

Quiz 19—b. ("David said to the young man who told him, 'Where are you from?' And he answered, 'I am the son of an alien, an Amalekite.' Then David said to him, 'How is it you were not afraid to stretch out your hand to destroy the LORD's anointed?' And David called one of the young men and said, 'Go, cut him down.'" 2 Samuel 1:13 NASB)

Quiz 20—b. ("Let not my lord, I pray you, regard this foolish and wicked fellow Nabal, for as his name is, so is he—Nabal [foolish, wicked] is his name, and folly is with him." 1 Samuel 25:25 AMP)

Quiz 21—b. (". . .and sent word through Nathan the prophet that they should name him Jedidiah (which means 'beloved of the LORD'), as the LORD had commanded." 2 Samuel 12:25 NLT)

Quiz 22—d. ("So Absalom's servants set fire to the field. That got him moving—Joab came to Absalom at home and said, 'Why did your servants set my field on fire?'" 2 Samuel 14:30 MSG)

Quiz 23—b. ("He built the Palace of the Forest of Lebanon a hundred cubits long, fifty wide and thirty high, with four rows of cedar columns supporting trimmed cedar beams." 1 Kings 7:2 NIV)

Quiz 24—c. ("Adoniram was in charge of the forced labor, and Rehoboam sent him to talk to the people. But they stoned him to death." 1 Kings 12:18 CEV)

Quiz 25—a. ("And when he had consulted with the people, he appointed singers unto the LORD, and that should praise the beauty of holiness, as they went out before the army." 2 Chronicles 20:21 KJV)

Quiz 26—c. ("And it came to pass after these things that Naboth the Jezreelite had a vineyard which was in Jezreel, next to the palace of Ahab king of Samaria. So Ahab spoke to Naboth, saying, 'Give me your vineyard, that I may have it for a vegetable garden.'" 1 Kings 21:1–2 NKJV)

Quiz 27—c. ("The angel of the LORD came again a second time and touched him and said, 'Arise, eat, because the journey is too great for you.'" 1 Kings 19:7 NASB)

Quiz 28—a. ("When Ahaziah king of Judah saw this, he fled by the way of the garden house. Jehu followed him and said, Smite him also in the chariot. And they did so at the ascent to Gur, which is by Ibleam. And [Ahaziah] fled to Megiddo and died there." 2 Kings 9:27 AMP)

Quiz 29—a. ("Then Naaman said. . .'may the LORD pardon me in this one thing: When my master the king goes into the temple of the god Rimmon to worship there and leans on my arm, may the LORD pardon me when I bow, too.'" 2 Kings 5:17–18 NLT)

Quiz 30—c. ("The people poured into the temple of Baal and tore it down, smashing altar and images to smithereens. They killed Mattan the priest in front of the altar." 2 Kings 11:18 MSG)

Quiz 31—b. ("These are more proverbs of Solomon, compiled by the men of Hezekiah king of Judah. . ." Proverbs 25:1 NIV)

Quiz 32—a. ("And he read therein before the street that was before the water gate from the morning until midday, before the men and the women, and those that could understand." Nehemiah 8:3 KJV)

Quiz 33—a. ("Esther had a servant named Hathach, who had been given to her by the king." Esther 4:5 CEV)

Quiz 34—c. ("And he took him a potsherd to scrape himself withal; and he sat down among the ashes." Job 2:8 KJV)

Quiz 35—d. ("How art thou fallen from heaven, O Lucifer, son of the morning! how art thou cut down to the ground, which didst weaken the nations!" Isaiah 14:12 KJV)

Quiz 36—b. ("Now Pashhur the son of Immer, the priest who was also chief governor in the house of the LORD, heard that Jeremiah prophesied these things. Then Pashhur struck Jeremiah the prophet, and put him in the stocks." Jeremiah 20:1–2 NKJV)

Quiz 37—c. ("Son of man, I have appointed you a watchman to the house of Israel; whenever you hear a word from My mouth, warn them from Me." Ezekiel 3:17 NASB)

Quiz 38—a. ("The visions of my head [as I lay] on my bed were these: I saw, and behold, [there was] a tree in the midst of the earth, and its height was great." Daniel 4:10 AMP)

Quiz 39—c. ("This time Jonah obeyed the LORD's command and went to Nineveh, a city so large that it took three days to see it all." Jonah 3:3 NLT)

Quiz 40—d. ("Meanwhile, the congregation waiting for Zachariah was getting restless, wondering what was keeping him so long in the sanctuary. When he came out and couldn't speak, they knew he had seen a vision. He continued speechless and had to use sign language with the people." Luke 1:21–22 MSG)

Quiz 41—d. ("John's clothes were made of camel's hair, and he had a leather belt around his waist. His food was locusts and wild honey." Matthew 3:4 NIV)

Quiz 42—c. ("There were fourteen generations from Abraham to David. There were also fourteen from David to the exile in

Babylonia and fourteen more to the birth of the Messiah." Matthew 1:17 CEV)

Quiz 43—a. ("But Herod the tetrarch, being reproved by him for Herodias his brother Philip's wife, and for all the evils which Herod had done. . ." Luke 3:19 KJV)

Quiz 44—d. ("But so that we may not cause offense, go to the lake and throw out your line. Take the first fish you catch; open its mouth and you will find a four-drachma coin. Take it and give it to them for my tax and yours." Matthew 17:27 NIV)

Quiz 45—b. ("Jesus answered: Not just seven times, but seventy-seven times!" Matthew 18:22 CEV)

Quiz 46—d. ("And when he had considered the thing, he came to the house of Mary the mother of John, whose surname was Mark." Acts 12:12 KJV)

Quiz 47—a. ("And behold, there was a woman who had a spirit of infirmity eighteen years, and was bent over and could in no way raise herself up." Luke 13:11 NKJV)

Quiz 48—c. ("I said to them, 'If it is good In your sight, give me my wages; but if not, never mind!' So they weighed out thirty shekels of silver as my wages." Zechariah 11:12 NASB)

Quiz 49—a. ("And now, behold, the hand of the Lord is upon you, and you will be blind, [so blind that you will be] unable to see the sun for a time." Acts 13:11 AMP)

Quiz 50—c. ("'I don't have a husband,' the woman replied. Jesus said, 'You're right! You don't have a husband—for you have had five husbands, and you aren't even married to the man you're living with now. You certainly spoke the truth!'" John 4:17–18 NLT)

Question 6

Quiz 1—c. ("These are the records of the generations of Noah. Noah was a righteous man, blameless in his time; Noah walked with God." Genesis 6:9 NASB)

Quiz 2—b. ("For example, Sarah obeyed Abraham and called him her master. You are her true children, if you do right and don't let anything frighten you." 1 Peter 3:6 CEV)

Quiz 3—c. ("And Abraham called the name of the place, The-Lord-Will-Provide; as it is said to this day, "In the Mount of the Lord it shall be provided." Genesis 22:14 NASB)

Quiz 4—c. ("The sun was risen upon the earth when Lot entered into Zoar." Genesis 19:23 KJV)

Quiz 5—d. ("Then he said, 'Is he not rightly named Jacob, for he has supplanted me these two times? He took away my birthright, and behold, now he has taken away my blessing.'" Genesis 27:36 NASB)

Quiz 6—a. ("Jacob, however, took fresh-cut branches from poplar, almond and plane trees and made white stripes on them by peeling the bark and exposing the white inner wood of the branches." Genesis 30:37 NIV)

Quiz 7—c. ("Two years later the king of Egypt dreamed he was standing beside the Nile River. Suddenly, seven fat, healthy cows came up from the river and started eating grass along the bank. Then seven ugly, skinny cows came up out of the river and ate the fat, healthy cows. . . ." Genesis 41:1–7 CEV)

Quiz 8—a. ("The magicians tried by their enchantments and secret arts to bring forth gnats or mosquitoes, but they could not; and there were gnats or mosquitoes on man and beast." Exodus 8:18 NASB)

Quiz 9—b. ("So that place was called Kibroth-hattaavah (which means 'graves of gluttony') because there they buried the people who had craved meat from Egypt." Numbers 11:34 NLT)

Quiz 10—a. ("Balak son of Zippor learned of all that Israel had done to the Amorites." Numbers 22:2 MSG)

Quiz 11—c. ("Then Moses climbed Mount Nebo from the plains of Moab to the top of Pisgah, across from Jericho. There the LORD showed him the whole land—from Gilead to Dan." Deuteronomy 34:1 NIV)

Quiz 12—d. ("The LORD had said that everything in Jericho belonged to him. But Achan from the Judah tribe took some of the things from Jericho for himself. And so the LORD was angry with the Israelites, because one of them had disobeyed him." Joshua 7:1 CEV)

Quiz 13—c. ("And Gideon had threescore and ten sons of his body begotten: for he had many wives. And his concubine that was in Shechem, she also bare him a son, whose name he called Abimelech." Judges 8:30–31 KJV)

Quiz 14—a. ("Now it happened at midnight that the man was startled, and turned himself; and there, a woman was lying at his feet. And he said, 'Who are you?' So she answered, 'I am Ruth, your maidservant. Take your maidservant under your wing, for you are a close relative.'" Ruth 3:8–9 NKJV)

Quiz 15—b. ("It happened at that time as Eli was lying down in his place (now his eyesight had begun to grow dim and he could not see well). . ." 1 Samuel 3:2 NASB)

Quiz 16—b. ("The donkeys of Kish, Saul's father, were lost. Kish said to Saul, Take a servant with you and go, look for the donkeys." 1 Samuel 9:3 AMP)

Quiz 17—c. ("So when the time came for Saul to give his daughter Merab in marriage to David, he gave her instead to Adriel, a man from Meholah." 1 Samuel 18:19 NLT)

Quiz 18—b. ("Then David ran up to the Philistine and stood over him, pulled the giant's sword from its sheath, and finished the job by cutting off his head." 1 Samuel 17:51 MSG)

Quiz 19—a. ("He commanded that it be taught to the people of Judah. It is known as the Song of the Bow, and it is recorded in The Book of Jashar." 2 Samuel 1:18 NLT)

Quiz 20—a. ("Sons were born to David in Hebron: His firstborn was Amnon the son of Ahinoam of Jezreel." 2 Samuel 3:2 NIV)

Quiz 21—b. ("When you get there, Zadok and Nathan will make Solomon the new king of Israel. Then after the ceremony is over, have someone blow a trumpet and tell everyone to shout, 'Long live King Solomon!'" 1 Kings 1:34 CEV)

Quiz 22—c. ("And Absalom and all the men of Israel said, The counsel of Hushai the Archite is better than the counsel of Ahithophel. For the LORD had appointed to defeat the good counsel of Ahithophel, to the intent that the LORD might bring evil upon Absalom." 2 Samuel 17:14 KJV)

Quiz 23—d. ("The king had a fleet of trading ships at sea along with the ships of Hiram. Once every three years it returned, carrying gold, silver and ivory, and apes and baboons." 1 Kings 10:22 NIV)

Quiz 24—a. ("And when Rehoboam came to Jerusalem, he assembled all the house of Judah with the tribe of Benjamin, one hundred and eighty thousand chosen men who were warriors, to fight against the house of Israel, that he might restore the kingdom to Rehoboam the son of Solomon." 1 Kings 12:21 NKJV)

Quiz 25—c. ("When they began singing and praising, the LORD set ambushes against the sons of Ammon, Moab and Mount Seir, who had come against Judah; so they were routed. For the sons of Ammon and Moab rose up against the inhabitants of Mount Seir destroying them completely; and when they had finished with the inhabitants of Seir, they helped to destroy one another." 2 Chronicles 20:22–23 NASB)

Quiz 26—b. ("But a certain man drew a bow at a venture and smote [Ahab] the king of Israel between the joints of the armor. So he said to the driver of his chariot, Turn around and carry me out of the army, for I am wounded. The battle increased that day, and [Ahab] the king was propped up in his chariot facing the Syrians, and at nightfall he died. . . ." 1 Kings 22:34–37 AMP)

Quiz 27—d. ("So Elijah went and found Elisha son of Shaphat plowing a field." 1 Kings 19:19 NLT)

Quiz 28—b. ("In the twenty-sixth year of Asa king of Judah, Elah son of Baasha began his rule. He was king in Tirzah only two years. One day when he was at the house of Arza the palace manager, drinking himself drunk, Zimri, captain of half his chariot-force, conspired against him. Zimri slipped in, knocked Elah to the ground, and killed him. This happened in the twenty-seventh year of Asa king of Judah. Zimri then became the king." 1 Kings 16:10 MSG)

Quiz 29—b. ("Gehazi, the servant of Elisha the man of God, said to himself, 'My master was too easy on Naaman, this Aramean, by not accepting from him what he brought. As surely as the LORD lives, I will run after him and get something from him.'" 2 Kings 5:20 NIV)

Quiz 30—b. ("Jehoiada found a wooden box; he cut a hole in the top of it and set it on the right side of the altar where people went into the temple. Whenever someone gave money to the temple, the priests guarding the entrance would put it into this box." 2 Kings 12:9 CEV)

Quiz 31—b. ("And Isaiah said, Take a lump of figs. And they took and laid it on the boil, and he recovered." 2 Kings 20:7 KJV)

Quiz 32—d. ("So the whole assembly of those who had returned from the captivity made booths and sat under the booths; for since the days of Joshua the son of Nun until that day the children of Israel had not done so. And there was very great gladness." Nehemiah 8:17 NKJV)

Quiz 33—a. ("Haman controlled himself, however, went to his house and sent for his friends and his wife Zeresh." Esther 5:10 NASB)

Quiz 34—d. ("Then said his wife unto him, Dost thou still retain thine integrity? curse God, and die." Job 2:9 KJV)

Quiz 35—b. ("You will keep in perfect peace those whose minds are steadfast, because they trust in you." Isaiah 26:3 NIV)

Quiz 36—c. ("The Lord showed me [in a vision] two baskets of figs set before the temple of the Lord. One basket had very good figs, like the figs that are first ripe; but the other basket had very bad figs, so bad that they could not be eaten." Jeremiah 24:1–2 AMP)

Quiz 37—b. ("He reached out what seemed to be a hand and took me by the hair. Then the Spirit lifted me up into the sky and transported me to Jerusalem in a vision from God." Ezekiel 8:3 NLT)

Quiz 38—c. ("It happened at once. Nebuchadnezzar was driven out of human company, ate grass like an ox, and was soaked in heaven's dew. His hair grew like the feathers of an eagle and his nails like the claws of a hawk." Daniel 4:33 MSG)

Quiz 39—b. ("On the day Jonah entered the city, he shouted to the crowds: 'Forty days from now Nineveh will be destroyed!'" Jonah 3:4 NLT)

Quiz 40—b. ("After this his wife Elizabeth became pregnant and for five months remained in seclusion." Luke 1:24 NIV)

Quiz 41—a. ("Jesus left Galilee and went to the Jordan River to be baptized by John." Matthew 3:13 CEV)

Quiz 42—d. ("Is not this the carpenter's son? is not his mother called Mary? and his brethren, James, and Joses, and Simon, and Judas?" Matthew 13:55 KJV)

Quiz 43—d. ("For Herod had laid hold of John and bound him, and put him in prison for the sake of Herodias, his brother Philip's wife." Matthew 14:3 NKJV)

Quiz 44—d. ("Now Philip was from Bethsaida, of the city of Andrew and Peter." John 1:44 NASB)

Quiz 45—b. ("She will bear a Son, and you shall call His name Jesus [the Greek form of the Hebrew Joshua, which means Savior], for He will save His people from their sins." Matthew 1:21 AMP)

Quiz 46—c. ("For instance, there was Joseph, the one the apostles nicknamed Barnabas (which means 'Son of Encouragement')." Acts 4:36 NLT)

Quiz 47—b. ("There once was a rich man, expensively dressed in the latest fashions, wasting his days in conspicuous consumption. A poor man named Lazarus, covered with sores, had been dumped on his doorstep." Luke 16:19–20 MSG)

Quiz 48—a. ("And he promised, and sought opportunity to betray him unto them in the absence of the multitude." Luke 22:6 KJV)

Quiz 49—d. ("For as I walked around and looked carefully at your objects of worship, I even found an altar with this inscription: TO AN UNKNOWN GOD. So you are ignorant of the very thing you worship—and this is what I am going to proclaim to you." Acts 17:23 NIV)

Quiz 50—b. ("Now there is in Jerusalem by the Sheep Gate a pool, which is called in Hebrew, Bethesda, having five porches. . . ." John 5:2–15 NKJV)

Question 7

Quiz 1—a. ("Now Cush became the father of Nimrod; he became a mighty one on the earth." Genesis 10:8 NASB)

Quiz 2—c. ("And in Hades (the realm of the dead), being in torment, he lifted up his eyes and saw Abraham far away, and Lazarus in his bosom." Luke 16:23 AMP)

Quiz 3—b. ("Without weakening in his faith, he faced the fact that his body was as good as dead—since he was about a hundred years old—and that Sarah's womb was also dead." Romans 4:19 NIV)

Quiz 4—d. ("Remember Lot's wife!" Luke 17:32 NIV)

Quiz 5—a. ("Nor because they are his descendants are they all Abraham's children. On the contrary, 'It is through Isaac that your offspring will be reckoned.'" Romans 9:7 NIV)

Quiz 6—d. ("And Jacob called the name of the place Peniel [the face of God], saying, For I have seen God face to face, and my life is spared and not snatched away." Genesis 32:30 AMP)

Quiz 7—b. ("But before Jacob gave them his blessing, he crossed his arms, putting his right hand on the head of Ephraim and his left hand on the head of Manasseh." Genesis 48:14 CEV)

Quiz 8—d. ("So Moses brought Israel from the Red sea, and they went out into the wilderness of Shur; and they went three days in the wilderness, and found no water. And when they came to Marah, they could not drink of the waters of Marah, for they were bitter. . . . And he cried unto the Lord; and the Lord shewed him a tree, which when he had cast into the waters, the waters were made sweet." Exodus 15:22–25 KJV)

Quiz 9—c. ("And when the cloud departed from above the tabernacle, suddenly Miriam became leprous, as white as snow. Then Aaron turned toward Miriam, and there she was, a leper." Numbers 12:10 NKJV)

Quiz 10—d. ("Just as Moses lifted up the snake in the wilderness, so the Son of Man must be lifted up." John 3:14 NIV)

Quiz 11—b. ("So Joshua blessed him and gave Hebron to Caleb the son of Jephunneh for an inheritance." Joshua 14:13 NASB)

Quiz 12—a. ("And the sun stood still, and the moon stayed, until the nation took vengeance upon their enemies. Is not this written in the Book of Jasher? So the sun stood still in the midst of the heavens and did not hasten to go down for about a whole day." Joshua 10:13 AMP)

Quiz 13—d. ("And Jephthah made a vow to the LORD. He said, 'If you give me victory over the Ammonites, I will give to the LORD whatever comes out of my house to meet me when I return in triumph. I will sacrifice it as a burnt offering'. . . . When Jephthah returned home to Mizpah, his daughter came out to meet him, playing on a tambourine and dancing for joy. She was his one and only child; he had no other sons or daughters. When he saw her, he tore his clothes in anguish. 'Oh, my daughter!' he cried out. 'You have completely destroyed me! You've brought disaster on me! For I have made a vow to the LORD, and I cannot take it back'. . . ." Judges 11:30–40 NLT)

Quiz 14—c. ("In the olden times in Israel, this is how they handled official business regarding matters of property and inheritance: a man would take off his shoe and give it to the other person. This was the same as an official seal or personal signature in Israel." Ruth 4:7 MSG)

Quiz 15—d. ("And it came to pass, when he made mention of the ark of God, that he fell from off the seat backward by the side of the gate, and his neck brake, and he died: for he was an old man, and heavy." 1 Samuel 4:18 KJV)

Quiz 16—d. ("Then Samuel took a stone and set it between Mizpah and Shen, and he called the name of it Ebenezer [stone of help], saying, Heretofore the Lord has helped us." 1 Samuel 7:12 AMP)

Quiz 17—b. ("Then Saul said, 'Thus you shall say to David: "The king does not desire any dowry but one hundred foreskins of the Philistines, to take vengeance on the king's enemies."' But Saul thought to make David fall by the hand of the Philistines." 1 Samuel 18:25 NKJV)

Quiz 18—d. ("Then David took the Philistine's head and brought it to Jerusalem." 1 Samuel 17:54 NASB)

Quiz 19—b. ("The next day, when the Philistines went out to strip the dead, they found the bodies of Saul and his three sons on Mount Gilboa." 1 Samuel 31:8 NLT)

Quiz 20—c. ("When David returned home to bless his household, Michal daughter of Saul came out to meet him and said, 'How the king of Israel has distinguished himself today, going around half-naked in full view of the slave girls of his servants as any vulgar fellow would!'" 2 Samuel 6:20 NIV)

Quiz 21—d. ("These things did Benaiah the son of Jehoiada, and had the name among three mighty men." 2 Samuel 23:22 KJV)

Quiz 22—b. ("Absalom ran into David's men, but was out in front of them riding his mule, when the mule ran under the branches of a huge oak tree. Absalom's head was caught in the oak and he was left dangling between heaven and earth, the mule running right out from under him." 2 Samuel 18:9 MSG)

Quiz 23—c. ("Unless the LORD builds the house, the builders labor in vain." Psalm 127:1 NIV)

Quiz 24—b. ("One day, Jeroboam started thinking, 'Everyone in Israel still goes to the temple in Jerusalem to offer sacrifices to the LORD. What if they become loyal to David's family again? They will kill me and accept Rehoboam as their king.' Jeroboam asked for advice and then made two gold statues of calves. He showed them to the people and said, 'Listen everyone! You won't have to go to Jerusalem to worship anymore. Here are your gods who rescued you from Egypt.'" 1 Kings 12:26–28 CEV)

Quiz 25—d. ("On the fourth day they assembled in the Valley of Beracah, where they praised the LORD. This is why it is called the Valley of Beracah to this day." 2 Chronicles 20:26 NIV)

Quiz 26—a. ("They washed the chariot at a pool in Samaria (where the prostitutes bathed), and the dogs licked up his blood, as the word of the LORD had declared." 1 Kings 22:38 NIV)

Quiz 27—b. ("And the LORD said unto him, Go, return on thy way to the wilderness of Damascus: and when thou comest, anoint Hazael to be king over Syria." 1 Kings 19:15 KJV)

Quiz 28—d. ("So it was, when the letter came to them, that they took the king's sons and slaughtered seventy persons, put their heads in baskets and sent them to him at Jezreel." 2 Kings 10:7 NKJV)

Quiz 29—d. ("But as one was felling a beam, the axe head fell into the water; and he cried out and said, 'Alas, my master! For it was borrowed.' Then the man of God said, 'Where did it fall?' And when he showed him the place, he cut off a stick and threw it in there, and made the iron float. He said, 'Take it up for yourself.' So he put out his hand and took it." 2 Kings 6:5–7 NASB)

Quiz 30—b. ("But Jehoiada became old and full of [the handicaps of great] age, and he died. He was 130 years old at his death." 2 Chronicles 24:15 AMP)

Quiz 31—c. ("So Isaiah the prophet asked the LORD to do this, and he caused the shadow to move ten steps backward on the sundial of Ahaz!" 2 Kings 20:11 NLT)

Quiz 32—b. ("I was cupbearer to the king." Nehemiah 1:11 MSG)

Quiz 33—d. ("The king took off his signet ring, which he had reclaimed from Haman, and presented it to Mordecai." Esther 8:2 NIV)

Quiz 34—c. ("Therefore take unto you now seven bullocks and seven rams, and go to my servant Job, and offer up for yourselves a burnt offering." Job 42:8 KJV)

Quiz 35—a. ("The LORD said to Cyrus, his chosen one: I have taken hold of your right hand to help you capture nations and remove kings from power." Isaiah 45:1 CEV)

Quiz 36—a. ("Then Hananiah the prophet took the yoke off the prophet Jeremiah's neck and broke it." Jeremiah 28:10 NKJV)

Quiz 37—d. ("And I will give them one heart, and put a new spirit within them. And I will take the heart of stone out of their flesh and give them a heart of flesh." Ezekiel 11:19 NASB)

Quiz 38—b. ("This is the inscription that was written: MENE, MENE, TEKEL, PARSIN." Daniel 5:25 NIV)

Quiz 39—d. ("But it displeased Jonah exceedingly and he was very angry." Jonah 4:1 AMP)

Quiz 40—c. ("When Herod was king of Judea, there was a Jewish priest named Zechariah. He was a member of the priestly order of Abijah, and his wife, Elizabeth, was also from the priestly line of Aaron." Luke 1:5 NLT)

Quiz 41—c. ("For John came neither eating nor drinking, and they say, 'He has a demon!'" Matthew 11:18 NASB)

Quiz 42—b. ("Jesus' father and mother were speechless with surprise at these words. Simeon went on to bless them. . . . Anna the prophetess was also there." Luke 2:34, 36 MSG)

Quiz 43—d. ("He had James, the brother of John, put to death with the sword." Acts 12:2 NIV)

Quiz 44—a. ("Simon Peter had brought along a sword. He now pulled it out and struck at the servant of the high priest. The servant's name was Malchus, and Peter cut off his right ear." John 18:10 CEV)

Quiz 45—c. (". . .Then he that had received the five talents went and traded with the same, and made them other five talents. And likewise he that had received two, he also gained other two." Matthew 25:14–17 KJV)

Quiz 46—a. ("But Paul disagreed strongly, since John Mark had deserted them in Pamphylia and had not continued with them in their work." Acts 15:38 NLT)

Quiz 47—c. ("While He was still speaking, a man from the house of the director of the synagogue came and said [to Jairus], Your daughter is dead; do not weary and trouble the Teacher any further. . . . And grasping her hand, He called, saying, Child, arise [from the sleep of death]! And her spirit returned [from death], and she arose immediately; and He directed that she should be given something to eat." Luke 8:49–55 AMP)

Quiz 48—b. (". . .the gang that had seized Jesus led him before Caiaphas the Chief Priest." Matthew 26:47–57 MSG)

Quiz 49—b. ("Seven sons of Sceva, a Jewish chief priest, were doing this." Acts 19:14 NIV)

Quiz 50—a. ("When Pilate heard this, he brought Jesus out. Then he sat down on the judge's bench at the place known as 'The Stone Pavement.' In Aramaic this pavement is called 'Gabbatha.'" John 19:13 CEV)

Question 8

Quiz 1—c. ("And Noah was five hundred years old: and Noah begat Shem, Ham, and Japheth." Genesis 5:32 KJV)

Quiz 2—b. ("The LORD appeared to Abraham near the great trees of Mamre while he was sitting at the entrance to his tent in the heat of the day. Abraham looked up and saw three men standing nearby." Genesis 18:1–2 NIV)

Quiz 3—a. ("For it is written that Abraham had two sons, one by the slave woman and the other by the free woman." Galatians 4:22 NIV)

Quiz 4—c. ("And if he rescued Lot, a righteous man, who was distressed by the depraved conduct of the lawless (for that righteous man, living among them day after day, was tormented in his righteous soul by the lawless deeds he saw and heard). . ." 2 Peter 2:7–8 NIV)

Quiz 5—c. ("Now you, brothers and sisters, like Isaac, are children of promise." Galatians 4:28 NIV)

Quiz 6—a. ("Then Israel entered Egypt; Jacob resided as a foreigner in the land of Ham." Psalm 105:23 NIV)

Quiz 7—c. ("And Joseph took an oath of the children of Israel, saying, God will surely visit you, and ye shall carry up my bones from hence." Genesis 50:25 KJV)

Quiz 8—b. ("Even to this day when Moses is read, a veil covers their hearts." 2 Corinthians 3:15 NIV)

Quiz 9—d. ("And the earth opened her mouth, and swallowed them up, and their houses, and all the men that appertained unto Korah, and all their goods." Numbers 16:32 KJV)

Quiz 10—c. ("Phinehas the son of Eleazar, the son of Aaron the priest, has turned back My wrath from the children of Israel, because he was zealous with My zeal among them, so that I did not consume the children of Israel in My zeal." Numbers 25:11 NKJV)

Quiz 11—d. ("And Caleb said, 'The one who attacks Kiriath-sepher and captures it, I will give him Achsah my daughter as a wife.'" Joshua 15:16 NASB)

Quiz 12—c. ("When they had finished dividing the land for inheritance by their boundaries, the Israelites gave an inheritance among them to Joshua son of Nun. According to the word of the Lord they gave him the city for which he asked—Timnath-serah in the hills of Ephraim. And he built the city and dwelt in it." Joshua 19:49–50 AMP)

Quiz 13—b. ("Then Manoah asked the angel of the LORD, 'What is your name?' . . . Manoah finally realized it was the angel of the LORD, and he said to his wife, 'We will certainly die, for we have seen God!' But his wife said, 'If the LORD were going to kill us, he wouldn't have accepted our burnt offering and grain offering. He wouldn't have appeared to us and told us this wonderful thing and done these miracles.' When her son was born, she named him Samson. And the LORD blessed him as he grew up." Judges 13:17–24 NLT)

Quiz 14—d. ("The town women said to Naomi, 'Blessed be GOD! He didn't leave you without family to carry on your life. May this baby grow up to be famous in Israel! He'll make you young again! He'll take care of you in old age. And this daughter-in-law who has brought him into the world and loves you so much, why, she's worth more to you than seven sons!'" Ruth 4:14–15 MSG)

Quiz 15—c. ("The wife of Phinehas was about to give birth. And soon after she heard that the sacred chest had been captured and that her husband and his father had died, her baby came. The birth was very hard, and she was dying. But the women taking care of her said, 'Don't be afraid—it's a boy!' She didn't pay any attention to them. Instead she kept thinking about losing her husband and her father-in-law. So she said, 'My son will be named Ichabod, because the glory of Israel left our country when the sacred chest was captured.'" 1 Samuel 4:19–22 CEV)

Quiz 16—c. ("And Samuel hacked Agag in pieces before the LORD in Gilgal." 1 Samuel 15:33 NKJV)

Quiz 17—d. ("So David took the spear and the cruse of water from Saul's bolster; and they gat them away, and no man saw it, nor knew it, neither awaked: for they were all asleep; because a deep sleep from the LORD was fallen upon them." 1 Samuel 26:12 KJV)

Quiz 18—c. ("Then the priest said, 'The sword of Goliath the Philistine, whom you killed in the valley of Elah, behold, it is wrapped in a cloth behind the ephod.'" 1 Samuel 21:9 NASB)

Quiz 19—d. ("Jonathan, Saul's son, had a son who was a cripple in his feet. He was five years old when the news came out of Jezreel [of the deaths] of Saul and Jonathan. And the boy's nurse took him up and fled; and in her haste, he fell and became lame. His name was Mephibosheth." 2 Samuel 4:4 AMP)

Quiz 20—d. ("'We don't have any regular bread,' the priest replied. 'But there is the holy bread. . . .' Since there was no other food available, the priest gave him the holy bread—the Bread of the Presence that was placed before the LORD in the Tabernacle." 1 Samuel 21:4–6 NLT)

Quiz 21—c. ("Then Zadok the priest, Nathan the prophet, Benaiah son of Jehoiada, and the king's personal bodyguard (the Kerethites and Pelethites) went down, mounted Solomon on King David's mule, and paraded with him to Gihon." 1 Kings 1:38 MSG)

Quiz 22—a. ("Absalom was still alive, so Joab took three spears and stuck them through Absalom's chest." 2 Samuel 18:14 CEV)

Quiz 23—a. (". . .vanity and vexation of spirit." Ecclesiastes 1:14; 2:11, 17, 26; 4:4, 16; 6:9 KJV)

Quiz 24—c. ("Rehoboam loved Maakah daughter of Absalom more than any of his other wives and concubines. In all, he had eighteen wives and sixty concubines, twenty-eight sons and sixty daughters." 2 Chronicles 11:21 NIV)

Quiz 25—c. ("And Jehoshaphat reigned over Judah: he was thirty and five years old when he began to reign, and he reigned twenty and five years in Jerusalem." 2 Chronicles 20:31 KJV)

Quiz 26—c. ("Then Jehu went to Jezreel. When Jezebel heard about it, she put on eye makeup, arranged her hair and looked out of a window." 2 Kings 9:30 NIV)

Quiz 27—a. ("Then it happened, as they continued on and talked, that suddenly a chariot of fire appeared with horses of fire, and separated the two of them; and Elijah went up by a whirlwind into heaven." 2 Kings 2:11 NKJV)

Quiz 28—b. ("Then Jehu gathered all the people and said to them, 'Ahab served Baal a little; Jehu will serve him much. Now, summon all the prophets of Baal, all his worshipers and all his priests; let no one be missing, for I have a great sacrifice for Baal; whoever is missing shall not live.' But Jehu did it in cunning, so that he might destroy the worshipers of Baal." 2 Kings 10:18–19 NASB)

Quiz 29—b. ("And when the Syrians came down to him, Elisha prayed to the Lord, Smite this people with blindness, I pray You. And God smote them with blindness, as Elisha asked." 2 Kings 6:18 AMP)

Quiz 30—d. ("Then the leaders plotted to kill Zechariah, and King Joash ordered that they stone him to death in the courtyard of the LORD's Temple." 2 Chronicles 24:21 NLT)

Quiz 31—d. ("Shortly after this, Merodach-Baladan, the son of Baladan king of Babylon, having heard that the king was sick, sent a get-well card and a gift to Hezekiah. Hezekiah was pleased and showed the messengers around the place—silver, gold, spices, aromatic oils, his stockpile of weapons—a guided tour of all his prized possessions. There wasn't a thing in his palace or kingdom that Hezekiah didn't show them." 2 Kings 20:12–13 MSG)

Quiz 32—a. ("When Sanballat, the governor of Samaria, heard that we were rebuilding the walls of Jerusalem, he became angry and started insulting our people." Nehemiah 4:1 CEV)

Quiz 33—d. ("And the king commanded it so to be done: and the decree was given at Shushan; and they hanged Haman's ten sons." Esther 9:14 KJV)

Quiz 34—b. ("And the LORD restored Job's losses when he prayed for his friends. Indeed the LORD gave Job twice as much as he had before." Job 42:10 NKJV)

Quiz 35—d. ("There is no peace for the wicked." Isaiah 48:22; 57:21 NASB)

Quiz 36—b. ("And I set before the sons of the house of the Rechabites pitchers full of wine, and cups, and I said to them, Drink wine. But they said, We will drink no wine, for Jonadab son of Rechab, our father, commanded us: You shall not drink wine, neither you nor your sons, forever." Jeremiah 35:5–6 AMP)

Quiz 37—c. ("Then he said to me, 'Prophesy to the breath; prophesy, son of man, and say to it, "This is what the Sovereign LORD says: Come, breath, from the four winds and breathe into these slain, that they may live."'" Ezekiel 37:9 NIV)

Quiz 38—c. ("It pleased Darius to set over the kingdom an hundred and twenty princes, which should be over the whole kingdom. . . . Then the king commanded, and they brought Daniel, and cast him into the den of lions. Now the king spake and said unto Daniel, Thy God whom thou servest continually, he will deliver thee." Daniel 6:1, 16 KJV)

Quiz 39—a. ("But as morning dawned the next day God prepared a worm, and it so damaged the plant that it withered." Jonah 4:7 NKJV)

Quiz 40—d. ("And Mary stayed with her about three months, and then returned to her home." Luke 1:56 NASB)

Quiz 41—d. ("And this is the testimony of John when the Jews sent priests and Levites to him from Jerusalem to ask him, Who are you?" John 1:19 AMP)

Quiz 42—d. ("Standing nearby were six stone water jars, used for Jewish ceremonial washing. Each could hold twenty to thirty gallons." John 2:6 NLT)

Quiz 43—b. ("And immediately the angel of the Lord smote him, because he gave not God the glory: and he was eaten of worms, and gave up the ghost." Acts 12:23 KJV)

Quiz 44—c. ("Jesus said, 'Bring some of the fish you've just caught.' Simon Peter joined them and pulled the net to shore—153 big fish! And even with all those fish, the net didn't rip." John 21:10–11 MSG)

Quiz 45—b. 28

Quiz 46—d. ("Aristarchus is in jail with me. He sends greetings to you, and so does Mark, the cousin of Barnabas." Colossians 4:10 CEV)

Quiz 47—d. ("Joanna the wife of Chuza, the manager of Herod's household. . ." Luke 8:3 NIV)

Quiz 48—a. ("Everyone in Jerusalem heard about this, so they called that field in their language Akeldama, that is, Field of Blood." Acts 1:19 NIV)

Quiz 49—c. ("And Paul dwelt two whole years in his own hired house, and received all that came in unto him." Acts 28:30 KJV)

Quiz 50—d. ("I, John, both your brother and companion in the tribulation and kingdom and patience of Jesus Christ, was on the island that is called Patmos for the word of God and for the testimony of Jesus Christ." Revelation 1:9 NKJV)

Question 9

Quiz 1—d. ("Now the whole earth used the same language and the same words. It came about as they journeyed east, that they found a plain in the land of Shinar and settled there. . . . They said, 'Come, let us build for ourselves a city, and a tower whose top will reach into heaven. . . .'" Genesis 11:1–5 NASB)

Quiz 2—c. ("The days of Abraham's life were 175 years." Genesis 25:7 AMP)

Quiz 3—d. ("Then Abraham buried his wife, Sarah, there in Canaan, in the cave of Machpelah, near Mamre (also called Hebron)." Genesis 23:19 NLT)

Quiz 4—a. ("Both daughters became pregnant by their father, Lot. The older daughter had a son and named him Moab, the ancestor of the present-day Moabites. The younger daughter had a son and named him Ben-Ammi, the ancestor of the present-day Ammonites." Genesis 19:36–38 MSG)

Quiz 5—b. ("Esau already had several wives, but he realized at last how much his father hated the Canaanite women. So he married Ishmael's daughter Mahalath." Genesis 28:8–10 CEV)

Quiz 6—b. ("Fear not, thou worm Jacob, and ye men of Israel; I will help thee, saith the LORD, and thy redeemer, the Holy One of Israel." Isaiah 41:14 KJV)

Quiz 7—a. (". . .of the tribe of Joseph twelve thousand were sealed. . ." Revelation 7:8 NKJV)

Quiz 8—c. ("But Michael the archangel, when he disputed with the devil and argued about the body of Moses, did not dare pronounce against him a railing judgment, but said, 'The Lord rebuke you!'" Jude 9 NASB)

Quiz 9—b. ("This [ark] contained a golden jar which held the manna and the rod of Aaron that sprouted and the [two stone] slabs of the covenant [bearing the Ten Commandments]." Hebrews 9:4 AMP)

Quiz 10—b. ("Now Joshua son of Nun was full of the spirit of wisdom, for Moses had laid his hands on him. So the people of Israel obeyed him, doing just as the LORD had commanded Moses." Deuteronomy 34:9 NLT)

Quiz 11—a. ("Caleb said, 'Whoever attacks Kiriath Sepher and takes it, I'll give my daughter Acsah to him as his wife.' Othniel son of Kenaz, Caleb's brother, took it; so Caleb gave him his daughter Acsah as his wife." Joshua 15:17 MSG)

Quiz 12—b. ("But if serving the LORD seems undesirable to you, then choose for yourselves this day whom you will serve, whether the gods your ancestors served beyond the Euphrates, or the gods of the Amorites, in whose land you are living. But as for me and my household, we will serve the LORD." Joshua 24:15 NIV)

Quiz 13—d. ("Samson answered her, 'If anyone ties me with seven fresh bowstrings that have not been dried, I'll become as weak as any other man.'" Judges 16:7 NIV)

Quiz 14—c. ("And Obed begat Jesse, and Jesse begat David." Ruth 4:22 KJV)

Quiz 15—b. ("So Solomon removed Abiathar from being priest to the LORD, that he might fulfill the word of the LORD which He spoke concerning the house of Eli at Shiloh." 1 Kings 2:27 NKJV)

Quiz 16—b. ("Then Saul said to his servants, 'Seek for me a woman who is a medium, that I may go to her and inquire of her.' And his servants said to him, 'Behold, there is a woman who is a medium at En-dor.'" 1 Samuel 28:7 NASB)

Quiz 17—c. ("And they put Saul's armor in the house of the Ashtaroth [the idols representing the female deities Ashtoreth and Asherah], and they fastened his body to the wall of Beth-shan." 1 Samuel 31:10 AMP; "And they put [Saul's] armor in the house of their gods and fastened his head in the temple of Dagon." 1 Chronicles 10:10 AMP)

Quiz 18—a. ("During another battle with the Philistines, Elhanan son of Jair killed Lahmi, the brother of Goliath of Gath. The handle of Lahmi's spear was as thick as a weaver's beam!" 1 Chronicles 20:5 NLT)

Quiz 19—c. ("He said, My lord O king, my servant [Ziba] deceived me; for I said, Saddle me the donkey that I may ride on it and go to the king, for your servant is lame [but he took the donkey and left without me]." 2 Samuel 19:26 AMP)

Quiz 20—a. ("But show kindness to the sons of Barzillai the Gileadite, and let them be among those who eat at your table; for they assisted me when I fled from Absalom your brother." 1 Kings 2:7 NASB)

Quiz 21—b. ("Then they played flutes and celebrated as they followed Solomon back to Jerusalem. They made so much noise that the ground shook." 1 Kings 1:40 CEV)

Quiz 22—a. ("But the king covered his face, and the king cried with a loud voice, O my son Absalom, O Absalom, my son, my son!" 2 Samuel 19:4 KJV)

Quiz 23—d. ("Come back, come back, O Shulammite; Come back, come back, that we may gaze at you!" Song of Solomon 6:13 NASB)

Quiz 24—d. ("And Rehoboam slept with his fathers, and was buried in the city of David: and Abijah his son reigned in his stead." 2 Chronicles 12:16 KJV)

Quiz 25—a. ("And Jehoshaphat rested with his fathers, and was buried with his fathers in the City of David. Then Jehoram his son reigned in his place." 2 Chronicles 21:1 NKJV)

Quiz 26—b. ("He said, 'Throw her down.' So they threw her down, and some of her blood was sprinkled on the wall and on the horses, and he trampled her under foot." 2 Kings 9:33 NASB)

Quiz 27—c. ("Elijah said to Elisha, Ask what I shall do for you before I am taken from you. And Elisha said, I pray you, let a double portion of your spirit be upon me." 2 Kings 2:9 AMP)

Quiz 28—d. ("In this way, Jehu destroyed every trace of Baal worship from Israel. He did not, however, destroy the gold calves at Bethel and Dan, with which Jeroboam son of Nebat had caused Israel to sin." 2 Kings 10:28–29 NLT)

Quiz 29—c. ("Then Elisha died and they buried him. Some time later, raiding bands of Moabites, as they often did, invaded the country. One day, some men were burying a man and spotted the raiders. They threw the man into Elisha's tomb and got away. When the body touched Elisha's bones, the man came alive, stood up, and walked out on his own two feet." 2 Kings 13:20–21 MSG)

Quiz 30—a. ("Joash was severely wounded during the battle, and as soon as the Syrians left Judah, two of his officials, Zabad and Jehozabad, decided to revenge the death of Zechariah. They plotted and killed Joash while he was in bed, recovering from his wounds." 2 Chronicles 24:25–26 CEV)

Quiz 31—a. ("Now the rest of the acts of Hezekiah—all his might, and how he made a pool and a tunnel and brought water into the city—are they not written in the book of the chronicles of the kings of Judah?" 2 Kings 20:20 NKJV)

Quiz 32—d. ("So the wall was finished in the twenty and fifth day of the month Elul, in fifty and two days." Nehemiah 6:15 KJV)

Quiz 33—b. ("Therefore they called these days Purim after the name of Pur." Esther 9:26 NASB)

Quiz 34—a. ("And he called the name of the first Jemimah, and the name of the second Keziah, and the name of the third Keren-happuch." Job 42:14 AMP)

Quiz 35—c. ("Thou shalt no more be termed Forsaken; neither shall thy land any more be termed Desolate: but thou shalt be called Hephzibah, and thy land Beulah: for the LORD delighteth in thee, and thy land shall be married." Isaiah 62:4 KJV)

Quiz 36—d. ("Then the king commanded Ebedmelech the Ethiopian, saying, Take from hence thirty men with thee, and take up Jeremiah the prophet out of the dungeon, before he die." Jeremiah 38:10 KJV)

Quiz 37—a. ("Again the word of the LORD came to me, saying, 'As for you, son of man, take a stick for yourself and write on it: "For Judah and for the children of Israel, his companions." Then take another stick and write on it, "For Joseph, the stick of Ephraim, and for all the house of Israel, his companions."'" Ezekiel 37:15–16 NKJV)

Quiz 38—b. ("I looked in the vision, and while I was looking I was in the citadel of Susa, which is in the province of Elam; and I looked in the vision and I myself was beside the Ulai Canal. Then I lifted my eyes and looked, and behold, a ram which had two horns was standing in front of the canal." Daniel 8:2–3 NASB)

Quiz 39—c. ("And should not I spare Nineveh, that great city, wherein are more than sixscore thousand persons that cannot discern between their right hand and their left hand; and also much cattle?" Jonah 4:11 KJV)

Quiz 40—a. ("And you, my child, will be called a prophet of the Most High; for you will go on before the Lord to prepare the way for him." Luke 1:76 NIV)

Quiz 41—b. ("The daughter of Herodias came in and danced for Herod and his guests. She pleased them so much that Herod said, 'Ask for anything, and it's yours! I swear that I will give you as much as half of my kingdom, if you want it.' The girl left and asked her mother, 'What do you think I should ask for?' Her mother answered, 'The head of John the Baptist!'" Mark 6:22–24 CEV)

Quiz 42—a. ("Now there stood by the cross of Jesus His mother, and His mother's sister, Mary the wife of Clopas, and Mary Magdalene." John 19:25 NKJV)

Quiz 43—c. ("So the next day Agrippa and Bernice approached with great display, and they went into the audience hall accompanied by the military commandants and the prominent citizens of the city. At the order of Festus Paul was brought in." Acts 25:23 AMP)

Quiz 44—c. ("One day Peter and John were going up to the temple at the time of prayer—at three in the afternoon. Now a man who was lame from birth was being carried to the temple gate called Beautiful, where he was put every day to beg from those going into the temple courts. . . . Then Peter said, 'Silver or gold I do not have, but what I do have I give you. In the name of Jesus Christ of Nazareth, walk'. . . . He jumped to his feet and began to walk." Acts 3:1–8 NIV)

Quiz 45—c. ("When they arrived, they went to the upstairs room of the house where they were staying. Here are the names of those who were present: Peter, John, James, Andrew, Philip, Thomas, Bartholomew, Matthew, James (son of Alphaeus), Simon (the Zealot), and Judas (son of James)." Acts 1:13 NLT)

Quiz 46—b. ("Only Luke is with me. Get Mark and bring him with you, because he is helpful to me in my ministry." 2 Timothy 4:11 NIV)

Quiz 47—d. ("And in all we were two hundred and seventy-six persons on the ship." Acts 27:37 NKJV)

Quiz 48—d. ("And they gave forth their lots; and the lot fell upon Matthias; and he was numbered with the eleven apostles." Acts 1:26 KJV)

Quiz 49—a. ("Circumcised when I was eight days old, of the race of Israel, of the tribe of Benjamin, a Hebrew [and the son of] Hebrews; as to the observance of the Law I was of [the party of] the Pharisees." Philippians 3:5 AMP)

Quiz 50—c. ("And I looked, and behold a pale horse: and his name that sat on him was Death." Revelation 6:8 KJV)